the man who
cured
the **perf⬤rmance**
review

**A practical and engaging
guide to perfecting the art of
performance conversation**

Graham Winter

JOSSEY-BASS
A Wiley Imprint
www.josseybass.com

To Carol, Mark and Ben

First published 2009 by Jossey-Bass
A Wiley imprint
www.josseybass.com

John Wiley & Sons Australia, Ltd
42 McDougall Street, Milton, Qld 4064

Office also in Melbourne

Typeset in Palatino LT 11/14.5pt

© Graham Winter 2009

The moral rights of the author have been asserted

National Library of Australia Cataloguing-in-Publication entry:

Author:	Winter, Graham
Title:	The man who cured the performance review : a practical and engaging guide to perfecting the art of performance conversation / Graham Winter.
ISBN:	9781742169514 (pbk.)
Subjects:	Employees — Rating of. Personnel management.
Dewey Number:	658.3125

Printed in Australia by Griffin Press

All people, companies and events in this fable are fictitious.

10 9 8 7 6 5 4 3 2 1

contents

part II: find the cause, find the cure

part III: the prescription

part IV: the cure

about the author

Graham Winter is a psychologist and consultant who has worked with top national and international leaders and teams in business and elite sport.

His appointments and experiences include:

- six years as exclusive designer and developer of high-performance leadership programs for PricewaterhouseCoopers Consulting in the Asia Pacific

- three-time chief psychologist for the Australian Olympic Team

- Director of Graham Winter Consulting

- author of the bestseller *think one team* (Jossey-Bass, 2008) and *High Performance Leadership* (John Wiley & Sons, 2002) designer of the think one team™ and cure the review™ frameworks.

Over the years Graham has worked with leaders and teams across the world, and saw the need to replace the often-ridiculed and ineffective performance review with something that fostered open and honest two-way conversations between people in the workplace.

Graham consults directly to corporations and through alliance partners who are certified to facilitate the think one team™ and cure the review™ frameworks. He lives with his wife, Carol, and sons, Mark and Ben, in Adelaide, South Australia.

Graham can be contacted through <www.curethereview.com> and <www.thinkoneteam.com>.

acknowledgements

Many people helped in so many different ways to bring this book and the cure the review™ framework to life; however, some deserve special thanks:

- Carolyn Turner for her wonderful coordination of the office that keeps our alliances and clients happy and allowed me the time to focus on getting the book and framework to the level we wanted

- Jo West and Elly Potter from West Creative for their always superb design work on the branding and resource materials

- Carol, Mark and Ben Winter for their never-ending support and love

- Ron Steiner for being a great example of how to give constructive feedback when I needed someone to tell me the truth

- Carolyn Mitchell and Julian Carne for their ideas and feedback on the manuscript and their support as clients over the years

- Frank Prez for his always professional guidance and advice

- Darren Coulter, Jo Kiley and the team at Karmabunny for their creativity in designing yet another great website

- Mr Sam Patten for putting me back together again after breaking my elbow on the day the draft manuscript was delivered

- the team at John Wiley & Sons Australia for all their energy and commitment to making this a great success

- all my clients, alliance partners and colleagues for their enthusiasm and willingness to help us replace those dreaded performance reviews with some meaningful performance conversations.

prologue

Can you imagine a less interesting topic than 'performance reviews'?

Try a word association test on a few colleagues. Chances are that you'll hear *boring, waste of time, pointless, damaging, bureaucratic* and maybe even *dangerous*. Ask ten people and the best you might get is *necessary*.

So, why write a book about performance reviews? And more importantly, why should you read it?

It began, as many things do, with a conversation.

As an Australian I spend many long nights on international plane flights heading towards places that sound exotic until you've travelled to them a few times.

On this occasion I was on Qantas flight QF11 Sydney to Los Angeles. The American in the seat next to me introduced himself and we struck up a conversation. As any regular traveller knows you don't want to spend fifteen hours sitting next to a 'talker', but we quickly found much in common.

Somehow, between the first and second movie, we got to talking about the frustrations of corporate life. I suggested that there were few, if any, things that consumed as many resources, damaged as many relationships and delivered as little value as the performance review.

The American nodded knowingly, smiled and asked if I knew the story of the man who cured the performance review.

Perhaps the wine and high altitude were affecting my new friend, but with curiosity piqued, and at 38 000 feet and 4.00 am Sydney time, I listened entranced to a funny yet compelling story that changed forever the way I think about those dreaded performance reviews.

He caught my attention with the opening line: 'Just imagine the possibilities of a team that had no fear of feedback'.

introduction

As the global financial crisis became a global recession the casualties started to mount. Banks, auto manufacturers, airlines and even entire industries buckled under the weight of falling demand, rising costs of credit and spiralling unemployment.

While some fell like wounded animals, others took advantage of the opportunities. This story is about one of the latter: Xmas Franchise Systems (XFS).

Headquartered in the United States and largely owned by unnamed financiers, XFS saw the opportunities early and snapped up a stocking-full of companies that could be linked together to create the total Christmas experience — toys, cards, wrapping, cakes, donuts, decorations, sweets and more.

XFS continued to grow into a substantial and profitable business. But when one extra piece was added the world was stunned.

recession-proof

Twelve months earlier Ralph Hampton Jr, Managing Director of XFS and the tenth wealthiest man in the US, had sat deep in conversation with a room full of his ever-grateful financiers.

'Own Christmas and we have a recession-proof value chain', promised the dynamic young businessman who had made his fortune growing a tiny gourmet donut store into a global franchise.

Some of the financiers whispered among themselves excitedly. Others rubbed their hands together. The boys from the vulture fund actually salivated. All agreed it was the most brilliantly conceived and perfectly timed strategy they had ever seen. Pull this off and they would all be rich.

And pull it off Ralph did, through a brazen acquisition of the world's most-loved franchise. Now, however, he was under pressure, real pressure, to deliver on the promise.

the world's most-loved franchise

It was two weeks before Christmas and, despite the economic gloom, across the shopping malls of the world an army of Santas sat patiently listening to millions of children eagerly placing their orders for the latest toys and games.

Suited in the traditional franchise uniform of red coat with fluffy white collar and cuffs, shiny black belt, snowy beard and polished boots, the Santas were identical and so was the question: 'Have you been good this year?'

'Yes, Santa. Can I have my game now?'

'Ho, ho, ho!'

It might have been 'Ho, ho, ho' in the shopping malls, but there was much less merriment back at the Lapland head office of Santa Enterprises, the world's most-loved franchise—and that was also to do with men in suits.

From the outside it looked like a typical mid December at Santa Enterprises. Everything buzzed with frantic activity. Toys poured from production workshops into the central supply chain warehouse, miles of brightly coloured Christmas paper all but buried the hapless Wrapping Department, the Sleigh Maintenance team argued over the finetuning of the famous sleigh and, as always, anxious reindeer handlers put Rudolph and his eight colleagues through a final workout.

streamline the business or else…

Only two things could disrupt Santa Enterprises. The first was unthinkable—an illness to Santa himself. This was unlikely, however, as Mrs Claus kept him well-sheltered from the chilly Arctic winds. And since accepting Ralph Hampton Jr's offer to buy the business the stress of managing the pre-Christmas rush was a thing of the past. A management team ran the franchise. He could just be merry.

The second wasn't unthinkable; it was inevitable. 'Not death, not taxes but performance reviews', grumbled Max, a Senior Toymaker with many Christmases under his ever-tightening yellow belt. 'Two weeks before Christmas, can you believe it?' he asked, not expecting an answer from his coworkers.

Indeed, the troubled XFS executive team, under pressure from nervous financiers to streamline the business, had chosen the week dubbed 'the edge of chaos' for the reviews.

No wonder staff chattered among themselves about finding another job, reindeer jumped skittishly sensing something was awry and team leaders, who detested performance reviews, did anything to avoid downloading the excruciatingly detailed forms.

Walking past the toy design workshop, Santa overheard one of the designers advising a young team member how to handle her performance review.

'Just sit and listen, and let your manager tell you what he thinks about your performance. Then make sure you tick every box on the form, agree to anything he asks about goals, because he'll forget it anyway, and then it will be at least six months before you have to do it again.'

Santa — or 'GM' (short for great man), as everyone called him — shook his head. It was never this way when he managed the business. As soon as Christmas was over he would speak to Brad Smyth, the newly appointed Chief Executive, because the hard-working folk of Santa Enterprises deserved better. And they would get better too, although certainly not in the way that Santa expected, when he became the man who cured the performance review.

part I

the review

chapter 1

hr harry and the perfect performance review

arry Robinson took over as Chief of Human Resources for Santa Enterprises at the time of the merger. Known to everyone (apart from himself) as HR Harry and reporting to the General Manager, Corporate Services, Harry was nearing the end of a thirty-year-plus career that began in Personnel and ended in Human Resources. He preferred Personnel and believed in running a tight ship. Harry liked to be well organised, expected his staff to be the same, always wore a tie (even on weekends) and prided himself on having the sharpest set of HR processes in the industry.

Like many of his colleagues at XFS head office, Harry firmly believed that one of the secrets to a well-functioning organisation was a thorough, meticulously managed and strictly applied performance review. When all he found at Santa Enterprises was what he described as 'an apology for a performance review' Harry dedicated every waking moment to his vision of creating the perfect performance review.

Shortly after the acquisition Harry had assembled a group of managers and team leaders for a two-day training workshop that would showcase his new performance review system and train these people to bring his vision to life.

'The performance review is a critical part of the whole performance cycle', explained Harry to a curious audience. 'The review will enable us to objectively evaluate the performance of all employees and then allocate pay rises in line with our budget.'

A sceptical manager from Sweets Division raised her hand. 'How can it be objective?' she asked.

Harry replied with an almost direct quote from the performance review manual: 'You will be using a well-researched checklist of behaviours and applying that standardised checklist to every employee. This rating and ranking of employees on well-defined scales gives us a complete set of metrics.'

Harry was full of jargon and pride; his colleagues thought he was full of something else.

'Rating and ranking? What's that?' queried a team leader from Warehousing who had been with Santa Enterprises for twenty years and had no idea what Harry was on about.

'Firstly, you will be rating your staff member', Harry replied, with extra emphasis on the word 'rating'. 'That rating will be from one—unacceptable—to five—outstanding.'

The manager nodded vaguely. He'd never seen a walking, talking procedures manual before.

'After completing ratings on all personnel you will enter these into the PMIRS, and then rank your employees so that management can identify the top and bottom ten per cent of performers.'

'What's PMIRS?', enquired someone.

HR Harry stood and felt tall. He knew his system was bulletproof.

'PMIRS is our Performance Management Information Recording System.' Someone scoffed loudly but Harry ploughed ahead resolutely. 'This state-of-the-art system not only provides all the forms and data analysis that you need, but will also speed up the review process by generating perfect phrases to describe staff when you fill in the PRFs.

'Oh, sorry, I should explain', he smiled smugly. 'PRFs are the performance review forms that you will download when needed.'

Georgie, Senior Team Leader in Wrapping, had heard enough. 'One of our suppliers has a system like that', she announced.

'And have they seen the benefits?' enquired HR Harry rather too optimistically.

Georgie giggled. 'Well, they reckon that everyone ends up with a "three" no matter what they do.'

'Why?' asked HR Harry more cautiously.

'It's like this', explained Georgie, enjoying being the centre of attention. 'Apparently no-one ever gives a "one" because you have to go through the pain of counselling someone, you can only give a "two" if the employee is new in the job, a "four" means the person is exceptional so you really shouldn't give many of those away or it blows the budget, and no-one has ever been given a "five". So they say it's completely useless!'

The whole room erupted in laughter.

Harry was exasperated but even more certain that these insolent managers and team leaders needed the discipline of the performance review to pull them into line.

'That sounds like a very badly managed system', he replied before yet another team leader jumped into the conversation.

'I've got a great team,' she said, 'so why do I have to rank some of them as poor performers?'

'Do we have an unlimited budget?' asked Harry.

There was a pause then a tentative reply: 'I guess not'.

'You guess not?' snarled Harry. 'Then how do you propose to allocate salary increases without an objective system to separate one person from another?'

The team leader wasn't ready to give up yet. 'I don't know', she replied sincerely, 'but giving people unfair performance evaluations will just wreck team spirit'.

There were nods and murmurs of support across the packed room.

Harry was losing patience, but ever the bureaucrat he sensed the need to reassure his audience.

'I have had many years' experience in the army', he began to audible groans, 'where there are some of the greatest examples of teamwork because of the discipline of rating and ranking of performance'.

Managers muttered loudly among themselves and more hands went up to ask questions.

'Enough', announced Harry. 'This company has been without the discipline of an effective performance review system for too long. There is substandard performance from many employees, and we owe it to our high-performing staff to provide them with feedback and reward.'

'No-one would disagree with that, but why does it have to be so complicated?' asked another voice from the back.

'It's not complicated, it's thorough', insisted Harry. 'And it will give you more authority to deal with employees.'

'Sounds good to me', announced Ted, Manager of Sleigh Maintenance and a recent draftee from another XFS business. 'I say we just get on with it.'

A few others nodded in unenthusiastic agreement, which gave Harry his lead to flick the first page of instructions for the PMIRS onto the projection screen.

As they read the first paragraph, the folk of Santa Enterprises wondered what had happened to the happy, friendly culture that Santa had created when he was the boss.

Xmas Franchise Systems
Santa Enterprises PMIRS Manual

In December all Santa Enterprises employees will be reviewed by their direct superior using the electronic PMIRS to provide the data needed for rating and ranking performance, establishing salary levels, apportioning bonuses and defining development activities. This objective electronic system will eliminate the bias of managers and employees and provide the information required by management to plan and execute the human resource strategy.

Harry J Robinson
Chief of Human Resources

---

seven reasons the performance review is ill

My American friend was a good storyteller and already had me jumping to the overhead locker in the plane to grab pen and paper to jot down some of the ills of the performance review that sounded so familiar.

seven reasons the performance review is ill *(cont'd)*

Are any of these a feature of your organisation? (Use the questionnaire that follows to assess the health of the performance review in your business.)

→ *Bureaucracy gone mad.* HR Harry is an extreme case, but so often management loses sight of the reason a review of performance can be valuable, and instead creates a complicated and unnecessarily time-consuming system. As a general guide, the more rules, the worse the system and consequently the greater the ridicule from the people who are supposed to use it.

→ *Feedback that is too late.* Any manager who is relying on a six-monthly or an annual performance review to provide feedback and manage performance issues is setting themselves up to fail.

→ *The platform doesn't fit the business.* The performance review platform will not be effective if it doesn't suit the business — in this case, the computer-based system. For example, one of my clients runs a trucking business and has an almost totally paper-based performance review system, which suits the hands-on, practical style of staff and the way the business operates. Another client, a high-technology manufacturer, has a system that is mostly online, and it works for this client because the staff are comfortable online and have ready access to a computer.

→ *One person's 'two' is another person's 'four'.* It's hard enough to get people to rate anything consistently on a one-to-five scale, but without clear definitions for each rating, and some common sense about using all the rating numbers, the end result becomes a farce.

→ *Ranking is for tennis players.* When Jack Welch, former CEO of General Electric, advocated the value in ranking people's performance and targeting the bottom ten per cent almost everyone rushed to copy this little gem. While no-one will question the need to improve poor performance, public ranking of people often damages the teamwork between managers and their direct reports.

→ *HR owns the review.* While HR continues to be seen as owner and guardian of the performance review it is likely to stay ill. Ownership of the performance planning and review system should be put in the hands of the people who will most benefit. HR should then partner with them to make it work.

→ *Unrealistic expectations of the review.* The performance review seems to suffer from schizophrenia. Some people expect it to deliver wonders, while others expect it to deliver nothing. We need to be realistic about what we want from the performance review before it can be cured.

questionnaire: check these seven ills in your business

	Yes	Somewhat	No
1 The performance review system is bureaucratic.	☐	☐	☐
2 There is too much reliance on annual or six-monthly performance reviews as a source of feedback.	☐	☐	☐
3 The platform for the performance review process doesn't suit our culture.	☐	☐	☐
4 The performance rating system in the review is ineffective.	☐	☐	☐

questionnaire: check these seven ills in your business *(cont'd)*

	Yes	Somewhat	No
5 We have a public ranking system as part of the review.	☐	☐	☐
6 Human Resources are owner, policeman and guardian for the review.	☐	☐	☐
7 There are unclear or unrealistic expectations of the review.	☐	☐	☐

Are there even more things not well with the review?

more ridicule than review

It was a ritual established long before Ralph Hampton Jr and his financiers decided that they could own Christmas. Every morning at 7.30 a small army of workers headed down the mushy tracks of snow and mud that led from their homes among the ridges and mist-shrouded gorges of Lapland towards the huge Sleigh Maintenance shed that lay on the outskirts of Santa's Village.

Known affectionately as the Sleigh Maintenance Guys they were hard at work in offices and small workshops spread around the inside walls of the shed, while a small team carefully dabbed paint on the magnificent sleigh that sat in the middle of the great shed.

Conspiratorial laughter seeped from the manager's office on the right. Two men sat at a computer, playing with the automatic phrasing tool that HR Harry had built into his performance review system. Like schoolboys about to launch a prank they sniggered while a printer sprang to life, revealing a partially completed performance review form strewn with words and phrases that described substandard performance:'Yet to come to grips with requirements','Needs immediate training','Unable to reach required height'.

They burst into laughter, jumped to their feet and exploded from the room, with Ted the Sleigh Maintenance Manager bellowing,'Where's Matt?'

'He's gone to do something in Cards', someone replied.

Without even acknowledging the reply, Ted, a man not to be crossed unless you liked a bit of misery, spun around and headed back into the office, tossing threatening words behind,'Tell him his performance review is at 11.00 am sharp or I'll fill the rest out for him'.

people are leaving

The cobblestone square in the middle of the village marked the exact centre of the valley, and it was here that Santa always paused to buy donuts from one of the many tiny cafes that framed the square. When he worried he liked to snack and today something was definitely worrying him, so two donuts were needed.

In the time it took to devour his favourite snacks Santa strode purposefully past rows of colourful workshops, towards the pride and joy of Xmas Franchise Systems—the brand new head office of Santa Enterprises. Ten stories high and equally as wide, it was constructed of large squares of dark tinted glass, interrupted only by a neon sign that flashed the jolly man's face day and night.

The'Glass Castle', as everyone called it, was custom built in super-quick time to suit the climate of Lapland and the wishes of Ralph Hampton Jr who expected what he called 'New York standard'. The Glass Castle was certainly that with its floor heating, automatic defrost windows, wireless broadband and work cubicles with white noise to hide distractions.

The great man was in a hurry as he walked across the marble-floored foyer, nodded to the security guard and rode one of the shiny elevators to a meeting room on the seventh floor, where he went to join a group of team leaders discussing their concerns about the Christmas eve schedule. Approaching the meeting room Santa heard raised voices and paused to listen.

'You did HR Harry's training course, Bert, so why are you so worried about doing the review?' asked a male voice.

'Because I got an email from one of my team and it's got a list of over twenty things he wants to talk about.'

'What's the problem with that?' asked the voice.

Bert's voice quavered slightly. 'It's like a set of demands and he's really having a go at me. Things like, "Why hasn't he had any feedback?", "I don't give the team any direction", "The salary's too low", "He doesn't get promoted because management doesn't like people who have fun", and so on.'

Someone else entered the conversation. 'That's ridiculous. You should just call him into your office and tell him to do his job properly or start looking elsewhere.'

'Why not just email him?' added another. 'My previous boss used to do that and it worked a treat. She'd tell people to take a hike without ever having to have the tough conversation.'

Bert tried to reason with his colleagues. 'Come on, guys. The review is supposed to be a chance for a chat with staff about their careers, not a blame game.'

'Not at XFS it's not', replied a female voice. 'It's their way of keeping control and with the bad economy it's even worse. Did you hear what Ted did to Matt?'

'No. What happened?' asked Bert.

'Ted gave him an ultimatum this morning to do his review at 11.00 or else.'

'Or else what?'

'Or else he'd do it without him. And you know Matt. He had made a commitment to help the Cards team sort out a problem with a new machine and he didn't want to let them down so he missed the 11.00 am timeslot. So Ted went ahead and filled out the review on HR Harry's whizbang software. You know the auto-fill part where it gives you phrases to paste into the forms? He put in Rudolph's details instead of Matt's, so the report says he's great at flying in formation, has a career aim to be chief reindeer, but needs more practise landing on high-pitched snow-covered roofs. It's pinned up in the canteen for fun.'

A few people laughed. Santa groaned. Matt was the best graduate engineer he'd seen in years. A future executive if these XFS people and their stupid review systems didn't force him to leave.

'I love review time', commented Lizzie, a mischievous team leader in Toy Division. 'Everyone sucks up to you in the weeks before their review.'

'That's fine for you,' announced yet another voice, 'but tomorrow I have to do reviews on a team that's had three managers in the past six months. I hardly know them. What am I supposed to do?'

That comment seemed to pep up Bert. 'Just do what my boss did yesterday and schedule everyone back-to-back for twenty minutes each. He talked rubbish, and then used the auto-fill in Harry's system to do all the paperwork.

I got through mine saying just three words: "Hello" and "Thank you".'

The great man had heard enough and walked into the room, interrupting the laughter about Bert's story. With none of his usual merriment he asked, 'Are some of you having trouble with the performance reviews?'

Silence. Heads down. No-one dared look him in the eye.

'Come on', he encouraged. 'You all know me, and the last thing I want is for people to be unhappy.'

Georgie jumped in. 'It's no problem, GM. We're just having a bit of a grumble, but what we really need to do is make sure that the Christmas eve schedule matches up against the Naughty and Nice list or there will be a problem', she said in the hope of changing the subject.

Santa wasn't convinced, but now wasn't the time to tackle the performance review.

'Is there a problem with the Naughty and Nice list?' he asked.

'There have been a few IT issues in the changeover to the ERP system', replied Bert.

'What's the ERP system?' asked a confused Santa.

'Oh, that's just a fancy name for the way the computers talk to each other', replied Georgie.

'At least, they are *supposed* to talk to each other', added Bert. 'But after the takeover the IT Department have had a lot of staff resign, and the Naughty and Nice team got a bit behind because XFS management changed the categories, so we just need to get things sorted.'

In all his years in management Santa had never heard of problems with the Naughty and Nice list, or of staff leaving, either. He had sold Santa Enterprises to XFS because it had become too much for him to handle the operations, particularly once the recession hit, and to keep people happy at the same time.

This wasn't the first time in recent weeks that he'd heard the business had problems and people were unhappy. He was sure that these damn performance reviews were partly to blame, but it was the comments about the Naughty and Nice list that left a particularly nasty feeling in the pit of his rather-too-large stomach.

should the review be on life support?

The review might yet be the tip of the iceberg of a bigger problem in Santa Enterprises, but it sounds like there are plenty of things wrong with a key process that XFS management is relying on to streamline a business that is starting to show signs of trouble.

Are any of the following symptoms part of your business practices? (Use the questionnaire that follows to assess your business against these symptoms.)

→ *Managers use the review to reinforce their status.* What is supposed to be a positive experience gets turned on its head by managers who use the review as a weapon to control staff and remind them who is the boss. When managers and team leaders play this status card it closes down conversations and devalues the whole process.

→ *The review damages relationships.* Relying on the review for feedback is almost inevitably going to cause fractured relationships. Trust is built on two-way openness, on treating each other with respect, having the tough conversations face-to-face and believing that the other person is competent. Does your performance review process really build trust or does it have the opposite effect?

→ *Reviews are done poorly by managers and team leaders.*
Too many people see the review as just an annoying
administrative process. But to do it well requires anything but
basic admin skills. If performance reviews are to be retained
as a business process, managers and team leaders need the
skills to build rapport, ask open and challenging questions,
listen, develop clear and shared goals, observe and give
feedback, and tackle issues that can often be emotional and
controversial.

→ *Reviews are done poorly by staff.* Most people haven't got a
clue how to get the most from their review. They don't know
how to prepare, they struggle to give feedback 'upwards', and
few are skilled at selling themselves and their ideas.

→ *Staff become disengaged.* Few things can disengage a staff
member as quickly and effectively as a manager not putting
importance on their review. Whether it is as bad as Ted's
treatment of Matt, or the twenty-minute burst described by
Bert, you don't have to ask too many people to find some who
think the way their manager handled (or didn't handle) their
performance review was disrespectful and a reason to reconsider
their contribution to the business.

→ *One way or the highway.* A one-way performance review simply
reinforces the old notion that the boss knows best. Businesses
cannot demand that staff turn up like primary school children at
a prescribed time to be told how they performed and then expect
them to be engaged.

→ *The performance review is ridiculed.* Ridicule is a consequence
of all the other ills. Yet from organisation to organisation people
ridicule the review as a waste of time and, in some cases, refer
to it as downright dangerous.

questionnaire: assess your business against these symptoms

	Yes	Somewhat	No
1 Managers use the review to reinforce their status.	☐	☐	☐
2 The review damages relationships between leaders and staff.	☐	☐	☐
3 Reviews are often done poorly by managers.	☐	☐	☐
4 Reviews are often done poorly by staff.	☐	☐	☐
5 Staff have become disengaged because of what happened with their review.	☐	☐	☐
6 Reviews tend to have one-way feedback.	☐	☐	☐
7 The review is ridiculed.	☐	☐	☐

Could the performance review really sabotage Christmas?

chapter 3

the night before christmas

The final days before Christmas were a blur of activity in Santa's village as despite the performance
reviews everyone did their very best to be ready for
Christmas eve.

With all that work behind them XFS Managing Director
Ralph Hampton Jr joined Mrs Claus, Santa Enterprises'
Chief Executive Brad Smyth and the Sleigh Maintenance
team to farewell the great man on the most important night
of the year.

Ralph had always enjoyed the corporate hospitality box
at major events but this one, even by his standards, was
something special as the fully laden sleigh headed by a
team of reindeer climbed high into the evening sky before
disappearing behind the moonlit hills of Lapland. In days

past the reindeer did all the work, but new propulsion technology meant that now they were really just for show.

During the night the Communications Centre would track the sleigh as it sped across the globe, refilling at strategically placed warehouses where the Supply Chain team had stored toys for the surrounding regions. Ralph would stay until midnight and then leave the management to Brad. That was what he paid him for.

another casualty of performance reviews?

It was five minutes until midnight when Santa noticed something was awry. He had been pushing hard between the far-flung cities of Australia, but the sleigh refused to reach full speed. In fact the further it flew into the darkening night the more sluggish it became.

Realising that Santa was falling further and further behind schedule the Communications Centre broke the usual radio silence to check what was happening. A worried Santa crackled across the airwaves and the Sleigh Maintenance team was summoned urgently.

'What can be causing the sleigh to lose power?' asked Brad of the assembled group.

Feet shuffled uneasily. Ralph glared at Ted. Ted glared at the mechanics. 'You guys did the final check, so if this goes wrong you're dead meat', he barked.

Ralph was pleased to see Ted was on top of things.

Brad gazed at Ted wondering what that was all about. 'I'm not interested in blame', he said bluntly. 'We need ideas and we need them fast.'

Ralph wondered if Brad really had what it takes to run Christmas.

No-one wanted Christmas to fail, but morale in Sleigh Maintenance had plummeted to new depths after Ted's round of performance reviews. None of them trusted him, or perhaps more accurately everyone feared him. They doubted that anyone would purposely sabotage the sleigh, but two of the brightest mechanics had left in the past month and just about everyone else had lost their passion for the job.

Matt thought of Santa out there in the darkness falling further and further behind schedule, all the while knowing that the rising sun was fast catching him.

'I've got an idea', announced the engineer.

'Let's hear it', encouraged Brad, while Ted looked angrily at this upstart graduate who didn't yet know who was boss.

'I need to check a couple of things with the GM. Can we get him on the line?'

'Sure', advised the radio operator, handing Matt a large set of earphones.

'What's this GM stuff?' Ralph whispered to Ted.

'The staff call him the "great man"', replied Ted sourly.

Ralph wasn't keen on one of *his* employees being called the 'Great Man', even if it was Santa Claus. And certainly not since *The Wall Street Journal* had used those exact words to describe him in a feature two months ago. He'd have Brad raise it in Santa's next performance review.

'GM, this is Matt.'

'Great to hear you', replied Santa.

'You too. Can you explain exactly how the propulsion system is behaving?'

'When I take off it's really sluggish, and then it slowly builds to about three quarters speed, but for some reason it just gradually slows down again as if the fuel isn't getting through.'

'Does the throttle still feel hard to push as it slows off or does it lighten up?'

'No, it's still hard.'

'Good, give me a moment to do some calculations.'

The mechanics chattered nervously among themselves, and Ralph compiled emails on his ever-present BlackBerry while the young engineer removed his earphones and jotted numbers on the whiteboard next to the communications console.

With the board almost full he heavily underlined two sets of numbers and put the headphones back on. Ted muttered something about a waste of time. Ralph quickly sent the emails. It might have been midnight on Christmas eve but if you worked for Ralph Hampton Jr the email wouldn't be a surprise. And it wouldn't be a Christmas greeting either.

'If we keep going at the same speed the dawn will catch you five hours before you are due to finish', Matt said to Santa. Everyone groaned. The children of Europe and North America would be without presents when they woke on Christmas morning. The magic of Santa Claus would be destroyed. Ralph Hampton would be ruined.

'However,' he continued, 'the basic acceleration is there so it shouldn't get any worse, which means I think we can make it if you are prepared to just use the propulsion for take-offs and for getting up to seventy-five per cent speed, and then use the reindeer to maintain the speed and for descents'.

'The reindeer', scoffed Ted loudly. 'The reindeer are for landings and for show. They haven't pulled a proper sled in ten years, and they're fat and lazy. Besides it's too dangerous to shut off the propulsion mid flight. You're wasting our time; just leave it to people who know what they're doing.' Ted had to finish with his usual put-down.

'Do you have a better idea?' asked Ralph bluntly.

'Er, no', replied Ted, caught unawares by Ralph who, when push came to shove, would always back an engineer over anyone else.

Meanwhile Santa knew the dangers, but he also knew his reindeer and the reindeer knew him. They would sense the loss of power and never let anything happen to him. It just might work.

Brad ignored Ted and Ralph; at least for now anyway.

'Santa, where are you landing next?'

'Budapest, Hungary. We have to refill the sleigh and there are still some hiccups with the Naughty and Nice list.'

'Another casualty of those damn performance reviews', thought Matt, recalling how productivity in IT had hit rock bottom straight after HR Harry piloted his beloved system on the hapless analysts.

'Okay, what if we try Matt's idea after the refill?' suggested Brad.

'Okay', replied Santa, who was already working the reigns to get the reindeer alert while in mid flight. Rudolph glanced back. The tug on the reigns reminded him of the old days when the reindeer worked harder than you could imagine throughout the whole night.

The historic buildings of Budapest rose out of the darkness as the sleigh glided towards a warehouse alongside the River Danube. A group of helpers quickly refilled the sleigh, gave Santa his next Naughty and Nice list, and held their breath and crossed every finger and toe as he soared back into the sky.

It took just under a minute to reach what he judged to be maximum speed. The Communications Centre was eerily quiet as in one motion he shut down the power and cracked the reigns. Instantly the reindeer leaped forward, not just maintaining speed but even lifting a little.

'Okay so far', he advised to relieved cheers from the Communications Centre.

As one hour sped into another the reindeer settled into the pattern of resting on landing and take-off before pulling again on the top of the arc and while coming into land. Santa skilfully spread the effort among the reindeer to avoid them tiring.

Ralph decided that his management presence was no longer needed, but before he left he took Brad aside and issued just one instruction. 'I want performance reviews on Ted and Mr Claus as a priority.'

the man who owned xmas

It was almost dawn when Santa delivered the last present and dashed back across the North Pole, leaving behind a night of stress and a world of happy children.

Brad greeted Santa and they walked together towards his cottage.

'That was a tough night', said the Chief Executive.

An exhausted Santa nodded. He knew it was caused by problems in Sleigh Maintenance. Maybe it was Ted or more likely that ridiculous performance review process that distracted everyone. He was too tired to think clearly.

Brad continued. 'It seems to me that we need some honest conversations in this place.'

Santa grimaced. He hated conflict.

Arriving at the cottage he turned to Brad and said what he had said year after year to anyone who would listen: 'I just want people to be happy'.

Brad smiled knowingly and left. There would be plenty of time in the coming weeks to do what had to be done.

Now was the time for Santa to drink his glass of milk and sleep deeply, dreaming of reindeer and full moons and the happiness of Christmases past.

Ralph Hampton Jr, on the other hand, was still awake: still sending emails, still planning how to streamline the business and how to reduce the sorts of risks he'd seen tonight, and still looking to truly reap the benefits. Now that he was the man who owned Christmas.

---

the business case against performance reviews

Performance reviews might not wreck Christmas, but they do wreak plenty of havoc across the business landscape.

Apart from the fact that reviews have an enormous cost in time and resources (and seem to be almost universally accepted without question), there are five other reasons, before going further to seek a cure, for considering whether it would be more humane to simply put the performance review to sleep for a very long time:

→ *Reviews damage relationships.* The typical performance review is a boss-initiated, administrative process, conducted at an inconvenient time, overly linked to the budget process and with often conflicting expectations from the participants. If you wanted to design a way to reduce trust between two people, this would be worth a look.

→ *Reviews lower productivity.* It is astounding how many people walk out of their performance reviews less motivated and therefore less engaged in the business because their boss did a poor job at the review. Imagine if the boss didn't have that opportunity.

→ *Reviews stimulate turnover.* I have interviewed numerous people who identified their performance review as the event

---

the business case against performance reviews *(cont'd)*

that precipitated a (successful) search for a new job where they might be more appreciated.

→ *Reviews reduce initiative.* Every business needs staff who show initiative but a morale-sapping performance review or the absence of any real feedback can stifle the creativity and energy of even the most motivated people.

→ *Reviews promise what they can't deliver.* Admittedly not every organisation claims that its performance review process ensures objectivity in allocating pay rises, but enough do to warrant a reality check. And that is that the corporate budget, when combined with the going rate in the market, has a significantly greater impact on individual salary level than the humble performance review.

Will the 'cure' be to abolish the review or is there a business case to keep it?

chapter 4

performance conversation

It was just five months since Brad Smyth, former chief of one of the world's most dynamic investment banks, had carried his stylish grey sports bag down the chiselled front stairs of his expensive New York apartment to a waiting limousine. After the mayhem of the financial crisis, Brad wanted to do something different, something a universe away from New York and investment banking. And he found it, or rather it found him, via the most unusual offer he had ever received from a head hunter. To fly to Lapland and take over the leadership of Santa Enterprises.

harsh reality — a business on the edge

Since waking from his customary Christmas morning nap, the normally jolly man had been moping around the house, driving Mrs Claus mad. Usually she could rely on him to celebrate Christmas with the elves until January 6 but this year he just stayed home, worried about the near disaster of Christmas eve and ate more and more donuts. Enough was enough. She phoned Brad's assistant. Could he meet Santa today? Yes, Brad would come over to the cottage after lunch.

Santa squirmed when she told him. He didn't want quarrels. Hated them. Preferred to wait until it sorted itself out.

They met in the garden, exchanged pleasantries and at Brad's suggestion strolled together along the winding track that circled the valley.

Brad was the first to speak. 'Santa, I have been in the job now for just shy of six months.' He paused. 'Normally I would have made substantial changes, particularly with the pressure from XFS, but I've been waiting until Christmas was over.'

Santa nodded, but his mind was already racing ahead. Substantial changes? What changes was Brad wanting to make? Ralph had promised no changes. It was supposed to be a friendly takeover. He wished he hadn't sold out. Sure, the business needed some tidying, but nothing too major.

Brad interrupted his thoughts. 'Let me be blunt. This business hasn't delivered on the promises Ralph made to the financiers. Profitability is too low, customer satisfaction is falling, licensing revenue is half of what it was last year, staff turnover in some departments is twice what it should be and the latest staff survey shows that people are disengaged.'

The great man's shoulders slumped. Brad continued. 'We have a great opportunity to blend the best of the cultures of XFS and Santa Enterprises and to build on our great brands, but it has to be done soon and, frankly, we all need to change for that to happen.'

'You mean me, don't you?' said Santa.

'Well, yes, I do', Brad replied sincerely. 'But I also mean me.

'Santa, the reality is that XFS is a cold, clinical business system that tolerates people at best. Santa Enterprises, on the other hand, is like a big family. But it is a company that doesn't like to deal with the harsh reality of things such as profit, performance reviews and efficiency.

'We haven't much time to find a way to get the right balance between the cold and clinical, and the nice and friendly, but if we don't, Ralph will put one of his business restructuring goons in charge and that will just kill the business. I think we should start with the performance review, even though it's just the tip of the iceberg, and I believe that you are the best person to do that.'

They stopped walking. Brad waited. Santa looked at him with concern. Birds chirped. Time passed. Finally Santa spoke. 'How would I create a performance review? I wouldn't even know where to start.'

'Well,' said Brad in typically relaxed but forthright style, 'I'm not asking you to create one because we really do have a good system, the issue is that no-one has the right performance conversations'.

'Which means the system by itself is worthless', added Santa, thinking out loud.

'Exactly.'

'But what about Harry?' asked Santa, not keen to cross the guardian of human resources processes.

'Leave him to me', replied Brad. 'I think you should have a good look at how other global companies are tackling their reviews and performance conversations because we aren't alone in these problems. There must be some things we can learn.'

It sounded inspiring. Santa thought for a few moments. 'Why don't you just tell us what to do, because I think you already know the answer.'

Brad half-nodded. 'You might be right, but sometimes just telling people what to do doesn't create the change that you need. I'll help you and give you every support, but you have the respect and the power to cure the ills of this company.'

Santa nodded. For some reason he trusted this man implicitly.

open and honest

On returning to the cottage Brad turned to Santa.'You'll need a companion to help you on this new project. I'm going to assign Georgie', he said.

'Georgie! Why Georgie? She's the most mischievous of all the team leaders', Santa exclaimed.

Brad laughed.'Exactly! She'll challenge all of us to make the performance review more than just another admin process that everyone blindly follows. See you tomorrow.'

The great man stood for a while at the cottage door wondering what had just happened. Mrs Claus peered through the window as a bunch of slightly drunk elves, celebrating the last day of Christmas, trundled noisily past the cottage cheering at Santa.

Eventually he turned and opened the door still thinking about Brad's feedback on the company that carried his name. No-one had ever had an open and honest performance conversation with him before. The truth hurt, yet he felt strangely relieved of a burden but didn't know why.Yet.

---

does the performance review really have a chance?

You don't need a business with Santa Claus in it to know that the performance review is not well.

Across the world managers use the performance review to bolster their status, HR builds ranking and rating systems to satisfy

---

the budget police and consultants make millions of dollars designing savvy systems for people to hide behind. The fact is, the performance review has become a sacrosanct bureaucratic process that damages relationships and disengages staff. The only time it seems to work is when smart managers and team leaders bypass the system and actually sit down with their staff and have real conversations.

At the same time, however, it is possible that the performance review is unfairly blamed for some things that are more about leadership and culture. Following are a few issues that can affect the success of the performance review.

→ *The review is a mirror of leadership and culture.* You don't need an MBA to know that some leaders put people first, some put tasks first, some do both and others just occupy the corner office. Common sense tells us that effective leaders are equally concerned about tasks and people; however, we have seen already that XFS management is mostly 'task-first', while Santa is clearly 'people-first'. It is unsurprising, then, that XFS has a rigid performance review process, while Santa Enterprises has taken it much less seriously.

This simple example highlights that in many businesses the performance review is more likely to be a mirror of the leadership practices and culture, rather than an administrative system with its own unique character.

→ *People are uncomfortable giving feedback.* People don't feel comfortable giving face-to-face feedback to other people in their workplace. You can tell people a thousand times to 'give more feedback', but in most cases they don't because they think it has more risks than upsides, and there is no mechanism other than the performance review (or perhaps anonymous surveys) for this unpalatable task.

→ *The purpose of the review is unclear.* Ask ten managers what they want to achieve from doing a performance review and at

does the performance review really have a chance? *(cont'd)*

least seven will mention improving staff performance. There's nothing wrong with that; however, ask the people being reviewed and the most common answers will be career development and salary increases. This means that unless managers are skilled in aligning expectations the review is potentially doomed from the start and aimed squarely at creating dissatisfaction for one or both parties.

Given all this, does the performance review really have a chance to succeed in your business? In the following questionnaire place a tick in the space between the descriptions that best represents the position.

questionnaire: check the health of the performance review in your business

	Set up to fail		We have hope		Set up to succeed	
Our management practices are skewed toward people-first or task-first.	☐	☐	☐	☐	☐	Our management practices place equal importance on people and task.
People are unwilling to give feedback.	☐	☐	☐	☐	☐	People are willing to give feedback.
The purpose of the review is unclear.	☐	☐	☐	☐	☐	The purpose of the review is clear and agreed by all parties.

Do you think the performance review is worth saving?

tick and flick

Four foot nothing tall, cheeky and clever, Georgie was the Senior Team Leader of the Wrapping Department.

Many people didn't appreciate that Georgie actually did a great job. Her staff loved her and no-one ever left Wrapping Department, but the more conservative managers resented the constant questioning about how to make things better.

Always first to pipe up with a comment at a meeting, Georgie didn't deserve a reputation as being difficult, and with a fresh set of eyes Brad quickly saw her charm and potential.

Brad, Georgie and Santa sat in Brad's expansive office on the top floor of the glass castle.

'Tell us what people really think of performance reviews', encouraged Brad.

Georgie needed little invitation.

'Where do I start?' she giggled. 'Well, it depends on where you work in the company. HR Harry thinks he's created the perfect system and that it fits everyone, but if you look at the company the only thing that everyone agrees on is that the performance review is more trouble than it's worth.

'Like in Sweets Division, Don the manager has never given anyone a bad review. Just last week he asked HR to sack two people for incompetence and when the HR people looked at the two reviews Don had rated both as "exceeded expectation".'

'What sort of comments were in those reviews?' asked Brad.

'Absolutely none', replied Georgie. 'Don's just a "tick and flick" guy.'

'What's "tick and flick"?' enquired Santa.

'He just ticks the boxes as fast as possible, gets his staff to agree and then hits the send button.'

'Wouldn't it be better if he wrote some comments?'

'Like the spin doctors?' Georgie chortled. 'Let me see', she said, taking her time to recall the best examples.

'Bert from Legal got a review that if I recall correctly described him as, "A team player, with strong social networks and exceptional presentation skills".'

'And what's wrong with that?'

'He's actually a heavy drinker, who bullshits a lot and buys people drinks to suck up to them.'

Georgie was enjoying herself. 'And then there's Sandeep who got, "A loyal and careful employee who is meticulous in his focus on detail". That really means he's a nitpicking procrastinator who can't get another job.'

'Okay, okay', chipped in Brad, seeing the funny side but realising the need to move on. 'From what you're saying, there's not much good to say about performance reviews in this company.'

'To be honest, boss, the whole system is sick. No disrespect GM, but lots of people didn't even bother to do the performance review when you were the boss. Now with this new system it's much worse, so from what I learned at the management training course we need to deal with the root causes and not just the symptoms.'

Brad was impressed. He always encouraged his teams to look for the real causes behind the symptoms because that was the only way to create lasting change.

'Any thoughts as to what those causes might be?'

'Well, people get surprises at their reviews, so I guess that could be caused by managers avoiding giving feedback, or maybe the system is just so complicated that no-one even bothers.'

world tour

Brad was pleased that he'd chosen Georgie to accompany Santa on his trip to find a cure for the performance review. They chatted for a while about companies they could visit to learn from. They decided on some key target companies and after a lively debate chose to include Donut Delicacies, the global franchise that set Ralph Hampton Jr on the path to setting up the XFS group of companies.

'I'll leave it to you both to make the arrangements', said Brad. 'All I ask is that you keep in mind what a mentor of mine once told me: find the cause, find the cure.'

'Excellent!' replied Georgie. 'We'll find it boss.'

Santa slumped in his chair. How could he possibly handle this incorrigible woman? And how was he going to explain to Mrs Claus that he was going on a world tour with a woman from the Wrapping Department?

Brad shook his head and laughed. Georgie was exactly what Santa needed to break out of his conventional thinking, although it would be anything but smooth sailing for the jolly man in the red suit.

Georgie was as blunt as she was relentless. 'We're going to need to disguise you, GM.'

He looked at Brad for help, but the CEO was already tilting his head sideways to study how they might disguise one of the world's best-known identities.

'I reckon the lemon detox diet for two weeks, a shave and a pair of Levi's', advised Georgie with an unnerving seriousness.

She already had a vision of Mr San Taclaus, a manager from XFS who was doing a study tour with his colleague Georgie.

Brad roared with laughter; Santa blushed with embarrassment.

Mrs Claus was surprisingly supportive of the whole idea, which was something of a disappointment to Santa who had harboured a faint hope that she might (mercifully) ban him from going. She even backed the idea of the lemon diet and remarkably within two weeks Santa had actually come in two notches on his big black belt.

The companies they had chosen would take them from Lapland through England to the United States, and then on to Asia and Australia. Of course HR Harry desperately wanted to be involved, but Brad had a private chat with him. It was one of Brad's trademark 'open and honest' conversations that had Harry doing some deep thinking about his career.

Just one month after their mid-January meeting in Brad's office and they were ready to go.

Santa looked in the mirror at Mr San Taclaus. He looked years younger without the fluffy white beard and the ten kilograms that had been shed from his bulky frame. They weren't exactly Levi's, but a neat pair of slacks, fashionable striped shirt and blue blazer made him look like any other middle-aged traveller of some wealth.

He walked out into the cold air to be greeted by Georgie with a friendly jab in the ribs. 'You look great, San.'

After a long hug from his dear wife and a handshake with Brad, Santa and Georgie were on their way long before the elves of Santa's Village came trooping out of the Lapland Hills.

---

six tactics to find a better way

No matter whether you intend to transform the performance review or change something else of significance in your business, the six strategies Brad is using to find a cure offer some great possibilities.

→ *Team curiosity with credibility.* Curious people such as Georgie who aren't afraid to question the status quo are ideal to get involved. It was a master stroke to team her with Santa who, despite being conservative and uncomfortable with change, is exactly the right person to sell others on the advantages of doing things differently. Georgie brings curiosity to find the better way and Santa has the credibility to sell it. This skill combination makes a great team.

→ *Find the root cause.* Brad knows from experience that a deeper search is the best chance to find a lasting cure. That is why he is providing the resources and the time to fix things properly, which gives hope that the cure will be more than just taking an aspirin and lying down.

six tactics to find a better way *(cont'd)*

→ *Encourage people to be open and honest.* Uncovering examples such as 'tick and flick' and 'spin doctors' highlights the sorts of silly practices that bureaucratic processes can foster.

→ *Suspend judgement.* It's only natural that we often go in search of solutions with some sort of answer already in our minds. Brad seems to know what he is looking for, but he is prepared to suspend judgement while others seek an even better way. Arguably the greatest advantage of this is that the solution will be customised to suit the real need.

→ *Look outside the fences.* Every company and every industry has a 'cultural fence', which holds in the core assumptions, norms and practices. Without this fence things would spin out of control due to too much change, but the search for a better way means getting around, over or through that fence.

→ *Have the courage to try something different.* We don't yet know what Santa and Georgie will find, but there is a sense that Brad has the courage to implement things that will genuinely upset the status quo. This final step is, of course, essential because without it no ideas or plans will ever see the light of day.

Try the following questionnaire to assess how your business goes about finding a better way.

questionnaire: how does your business find a better way?

	Yes	Somewhat	No
1 We build partnerships and teams that combine curiosity with credibility.	☐	☐	☐

	Yes	Somewhat	No
2 We allocate the time and resources to get to the root cause.	☐	☐	☐
3 We encourage people to be open and honest.	☐	☐	☐
4 We suspend judgement while people search for better ideas.	☐	☐	☐
5 We look outside the fence.	☐	☐	☐
6 We have the courage to try something different.	☐	☐	☐

Is there work to be done for you to prepare for change?

find the cause, find the cure

chapter 6

dancers and dumpers

T
he first stop on the world tour was London, England, with a visit to Send Cards!, one of the world's largest suppliers of Christmas and other greeting cards, and another of the XFS group of companies.

Under the guise of being business students conducting research on performance reviews, San Taclaus and Georgie were welcomed as guests. No-one had any idea that they were in the company of the great man himself.

Georgie was keen to get the insights of people who were on the receiving end of performance reviews, so their first workshop did not include any managers or team leaders.

The group of twenty-five people looked decidedly nervous as they sat around five tables waiting for the session to begin. There was nothing to worry about, however, as Santa's friendly style soon had comments on the Send Cards! performance reviews flying thick and fast, while

Georgie summarised them on the electronic whiteboard. Most were remarkably similar to what they had seen at Santa Enterprises: too bureaucratic; mostly 'tick and flick'; poorly handled by managers; unclear purpose; and, not surprisingly, a waste of time.

dancers

One of the more confident people in the group, a man whom Santa judged to be in his late forties, asked if he could draw something on the whiteboard.

'Sure', replied Georgie, pressing the forward button so that a clean screen rolled into view.

Despite wearing an old T-shirt and jeans the man had the distinguished look of a business professor as he walked confidently to the board and then turned to face the group.

'I've had twenty years' experience watching managers do performance reviews, and in all that time I have concluded that you can divide ninety per cent of them into two groups: the dancers and the dumpers.' He twisted slightly to write 'Dancers' in thick black pen on the top left and then 'Dumpers' on the top right of the whiteboard.

'The Professor', as Georgie dubbed him, had everyone's attention. 'Take my team leader. He's a classic dancer. When you sit down for your review he'll talk about anything but your review. Last year it was his holiday to Disneyworld and the merits of travelling with teenagers. Then he described the review as "an administrative requirement", and in less than ten minutes ticked all the boxes, got me to sign it and bustled me out of the office.'

A young woman sitting near the front jumped into the conversation. 'I think I've got a dancer too. My manager doesn't do any preparation or tell you that your review is going to happen. She just calls people in when she thinks they're in a good mood, prattles on about how you've done a good job and gets it over in fifteen minutes. She's never once given anyone a negative comment in their review.'

Heads nodded and conversations broke out in the group.

'You're lucky', complained a middle-aged man. 'I haven't had a review in three years, so I asked HR and found out that my boss just cut and pasted the previous review and submitted it without me even knowing.'

'My boss told me that someone in his previous company got sued for what they put on a review, so he just refuses to write any comments', noted another. 'He can't handle conflict. It's pathetic watching him dance around issues instead of confronting them.'

'I reckon we need to put our hands up too', suggested a young woman. 'Lots of staff use this dancing stuff to just get through the review as fast as possible and to duck any tough conversations.'

People agreed and there were many stories to share so they let the conversations flow for a while, and at the same time the Professor jotted short descriptions underneath the heading 'Dancers' on the whiteboard.

Dancers	Dumpers
Avoid tough conversations	
Only give positive feedback	
Dance around issues	
Rush the review	
Hide behind the system	
Never give feedback	

sugar coating

As the conversations started to die down Santa asked the Professor to share his thoughts on why people at all levels in the business acted as dancers.

'Dancers', he explained, 'are avoiders. There are lots of reasons for this, but mostly it's a combination of wanting to be liked, feeling insecure and being too afraid to give feedback in case it upsets people. Dancers do everything possible to avoid getting to the point at a review, and they never give people anything other than vague positive comments during the year. Everything is either "fine", "great" or "lovely", and when they don't like something they give hints but never have the honest conversation. They may tell other people but never the person directly'.

'So they sugar coat their feedback?' asked Georgie.

'Yeah, but that's probably at best because your classic dancer never even gets to feedback at all.'

The man continued. 'Ironically, doing performance reviews can actually suit some dancers because if they can't totally avoid the feedback conversation, then the more bureaucratic and detailed the format the easier it is the hide behind the system.'

He turned to Santa. 'Have you seen dancers in your company?'

Santa was deep in thought and didn't realise that the man was addressing him.

'Hey, San, wake up', Georgie called to the sound of laughter in the group.

Santa suddenly realised that he was the centre of attention.

'I wasn't asleep', he replied a little tersely. 'I was thinking.'

'What about?' she asked with customary bluntness.

The great man blushed.

'I just realised I'm a dancer', he replied, his voice tinged with a sad resignation that silenced the room. 'When I think back I guess I've never really given anyone feedback about something they can do better. The conversations are always about making people happy.'

dumpers

The Professor could see that their guest had recognised something inside himself.

'Don't be too hard on yourself. Most people are dancers until they learn how to have a feedback conversation, and being a dancer is a lot better than being a dumper.'

'What's a dumper?' asked Santa, somewhat relieved to shift the topic.

'Dumpers use the performance review to dump all the negative stuff that they don't have the courage or skills to talk about at other times.'

'Then my boss is an A-grade dumper', announced a voice from the back of the room to muffled laughter.

'He just keeps these little notes about what you do or don't do, and then at the review he brings them all out. At my last review he told me that six months earlier the graphs I prepared for the quality improvement team weren't up to standard and for the last three months I'd been arriving later than he expected. And do you know what? The turkey actually bought a copy of a book called *The Manager's Guide to Terminating Employees* and he sits it on his desk whenever he does a review so he can intimidate you.'

Georgie cracked up laughing while simultaneous conversations broke out around the room as people shared their 'dumper' stories.

'It sounds like dumpers dump at all different times', commented Santa.

'Absolutely', replied a female voice. 'I have two team leaders and one dumps at monthly team meetings, while the other holds it so she can dump on people at their review.'

The female voice continued more seriously. 'Let's be honest. Plenty of us use dumping as a weapon to scare off managers and people from other departments.' A few eyes diverted downwards suggesting that she had hit a raw nerve.

Again the Professor jotted everyone's comments on the whiteboard.

Dancers	Dumpers
Avoid tough conversations	Give surprises at reviews
Only give positive feedback	Deliver blunt feedback
Dance around issues	Wait until it suits them
Rush the review	Make the review one way
Hide behind the system	Tend to be negative
Never give feedback	

Again the Professor brought a touch of wisdom to the group.

'Control', he said in an assured tone. 'Dumpers like to control people and situations. Managers use their status to control the performance review, which means it's almost always one way and negative.'

People nodded. They could immediately see what he meant. Georgie thought of Ted in Sleigh Maintenance. 'What a dumper', she thought. It was why the whole team was so unhappy and mistrustful of him, and it also made her realise that some staff seemed to be copying his style as a way to defend themselves.

After further discussion Santa thanked everyone for their contribution and as they shuffled from the room he walked over to speak to the Professor.

The Professor was still a little concerned that Santa was upset from revealing himself as a dancer in front of the whole group.

'Are you okay about that?' he asked.

'Very much so', replied Santa. 'I think it explains the problems that I've had in trying to be a good manager while wanting everyone to be happy and to like me. And I've been doing the same thing with my boss since the merger.'

The Professor could see that Santa was fine, so they parted with his final words: 'Most people, whether or not they're managers, struggle to find that sweet spot between dancing and dumping. If you can find that, you'll be a long way towards curing the review.'

---

on dancers and dumpers

It's time for a bit of self-reflection. How do you handle performance reviews and other conversations (such as in business meetings) where there's a need to give feedback?

Take a look at the following questionnaire and for each item tick the box that best describes the way you tackle the issue and situation.

questionnaire: are you a dancer or a dumper?

		Never	Rarely	Some-times	Often	Always
1	When people do the wrong thing I tell them when and where it suits me.	☐	☐	☐	☐	☐
2	I tell people the way it is.	☐	☐	☐	☐	☐
3	At performance reviews I give feedback that surprises people.	☐	☐	☐	☐	☐
4	In meetings I give feedback that could surprise people.	☐	☐	☐	☐	☐
5	I sit behind my desk when doing performance reviews.	☐	☐	☐	☐	☐
6	When people perform poorly I wait to see if it sorts itself out.	☐	☐	☐	☐	☐
7	I don't give people clear feedback.	☐	☐	☐	☐	☐
8	At performance reviews I avoid discussing the tough issues.	☐	☐	☐	☐	☐
9	In meetings I avoid the tough conversations.	☐	☐	☐	☐	☐
10	I try to avoid conflict because it damages relationships.	☐	☐	☐	☐	☐

You can probably tell that items one to five are classic 'dumper' behaviour, so if you ticked 'Sometimes', 'Often' or 'Always' on any of these items, watch out that your bluntness might be giving people unpleasant surprises or damaging relationships instead of tackling the problems.

Items six to ten are 'dancer' behaviour, so if you ticked 'Sometimes', 'Often' or 'Always' you may be avoiding feedback conversations and instead dancing around issues and leaving things to run their own course.

Sometimes these types of behaviour will be the right way to act, but beware that it's not just a convenient excuse to avoid tackling the issue.

Take a look at the following questionnaire to assess whether you have found that 'sweet spot' between dancing and dumping.

questionnaire: have you found the sweet spot?

		Never	Rarely	Some-times	Often	Always
1	When people do the wrong thing I choose the right time and place to tell them.	☐	☐	☐	☐	☐
2	I do tackle the tough conversation—by being open and honest in a style that suits the person and the situation.	☐	☐	☐	☐	☐
3	At performance reviews I only cover issues that people have received feedback on before.	☐	☐	☐	☐	☐

questionnaire: have you found the sweet spot? *(cont'd)*

	Never	Rarely	Some-times	Often	Always
4 I tackle difficult issues by either raising them before meeting with the people concerned or raising them in a way that doesn't damage relationships.	☐	☐	☐	☐	☐
5 I sit next to people when doing performance reviews.	☐	☐	☐	☐	☐

Give yourself a pat on the back for any scores of 'Often or 'Always' because you are showing the courage and skill needed to tackle tough issues without using avoidance or power to make it easy on yourself.

Find the sweet spot between dancing and dumping.

the donut or the hole?

N ext stop: Orlando, Florida, and a visit to Donut Delicacies, the company that started Ralph Hampton Jr on the path to mega wealth.

It was the classic 'boy makes good' story. At ten years of age Ralph visited Disneyworld with his family and happened upon a tiny shop called Donut Delicacies on the outskirts of Orlando. The typical small business was family owned and sold Mrs Turner's mouth-watering gourmet donuts.

Ralph loved those donuts more than anything he'd ever tasted in his short life and he announced proudly to his family that when he grew up he was going to buy Donut Delicacies and grow it into the biggest and best donut company in the world with a shop on every street corner.

True to his word, on leaving university Ralph convinced a family friend in the venture capital business to be his partner and together they bought the Turner family's shop, recipes and curious orange donut logo. From there, one shop became two, the kitchen became a factory, two shops became a hundred and Ralph became very rich and very skilled in buying and building global franchises.

Now Ralph was too preoccupied to spend much time at his beloved Donut Delicacies, but he still had fresh donuts shipped every day to wherever he was in the world because life was too short to have even one morning tea without at least one of Mrs Turner's delicious delicacies.

bud eldon

After a quick tour of the modern office building the Operations Manager, Bud Eldon, led Santa and Georgie across a paved courtyard fringed by palm trees, before entering the factory where thousands of sweet-tasting, brightly coloured donuts poured out every day of the year.

Bud Eldon was part of a reshaped management team that had formed over the past few years as Ralph pursued his acquisition strategy. Six foot three inches tall, emotionless and with a deep gravelly voice that rolled out in a slow southern drawl, the controller of Operations moved through the factory like a truck through a crowd. Wherever Bud walked the people ten metres ahead scurried away or just ducked their heads as if cowering from a strong squall.

'I would have preferred that we started with a management meeting', announced Bud, without looking at his guests. 'But we've got some problems with a key customer, so while the boss is attending to that you'll spend the morning with the team leaders.' Georgie wondered whether Clint Eastwood might be available to play Bud in a movie if the opportunity arose.

Reaching the far end of the factory, they paused before entering the training room where twenty team leaders dressed in white overalls with the bright orange donut symbol on their pocket sat around a large U-shaped table and waited, as they often did, for the Head of Operations to arrive.

Bud scraped the ground with his steel-capped boot. 'You might find this group a bit negative.'

'Oh?' replied Santa quietly, for fear of being overheard by the people waiting in the room.

Bud continued with a tone and volume that suggested he either wanted the people in the room to hear him or he didn't care. 'Our team leaders have some of the best working conditions that you'll find in a long day's drive.' Georgie wasn't quite sure what driving had to do with Bud's observations, but she listened anyway. 'Seems to me that the more you give people the less satisfied they become and the worse they perform', mused Bud in his best drawl. 'Anyway, you'll hear more whingeing and problems than you need to know, so I can manage the meeting for you and make sure we keep things nice and positive', he suggested in a decidedly menacing tone that made Georgie glance to check if he might be armed.

'That won't be necessary, Mr Eldon', Georgie replied politely. 'We can handle the group.'

Bud looked down at the short blonde woman and shook his head, unconvinced. More than once Bud had told anyone in earshot that focus groups were about as much fun as funerals and as much use as a half-chewed donut. Anyway, he had more important things to do, so he accepted their view in return for a debrief as soon the meeting was over. They agreed and entered the room.

After introductions, Bud departed and Santa opened proceedings. 'Tell us about some of the things that you like about the performance review.'

Silence.

'Anything?' he enquired hopefully.

A few heads shook but most of the people in white overalls with orange donut logos just sat there.

'Why don't we start with what doesn't work, and then we can work up from there', interjected the always-optimistic Georgie.

'Okay', offered one of the female team leaders. 'Can I explain why no-one will speak?'

'Of course', replied the visitors in chorus.

'As you probably know, this company was started by Ralph Hampton Jr. He did a great job of building it up until about three years ago when he got distracted by his grand ambition and lost touch with the management of the business. He let Bud run the day-to-day business and we've hardly seen Phil Sprinkler, the new CEO, who started about eighteen months ago.

'You also know that we work for a donut company.' They nodded, thinking that was pretty obvious. 'And you've met Bud?' They nodded again as a murmur of amusement drifted across the room.

'This is now the sort of company where if you give a manager a donut, they'll demand to know who stole the hole!'

Georgie laughed loudly, while Santa, with concern, asked the team leader exactly what she meant.

'All the business systems from strategic planning to performance reviews are ridiculously detailed and negative.

Management is obsessed with finding out what happened to the damn donut hole. We could make the best donuts, hit double the budget target or achieve all our personal objectives and they'd still go looking for the hole.'

'Do you make the best donuts and hit double the budget?' enquired Georgie.

'Not anymore we don't', replied a man who was seated at the far end of the U-shaped table.

'We were the best, but people have lost the passion for the company and it's got a lot to do with the way they use those damn performance reviews as a weapon', commented a man seated at the far end of the table. Santa thought this sounded eerily familiar.

'I had my review with Bud last month', volunteered another male team leader who was so rotund that Georgie giggled at the thought that his job might have been donut taster.

'Bud turned up with my form already completed, told me that ninety-eight per cent of what I did was satisfactory and then spent sixty minutes going through everything that was wrong with Operations and how my two per cent was one of the causes.'

'What about discussing goals or development plans?' asked the ever-curious Georgie.

'You're kidding', said the man, still obviously angry about his review. 'The rocket scientists in HR created a checklist for the review that is so detailed there wasn't time at the end for anything other than Bud to give me a sheet of paper with my targets and get me to sign the form.'

'Do you know HR Harry?', she asked to blank looks.

'What's in the checklist?' asked Santa.

'You name it and it's in there', replied another team leader. 'Apart from everything they paste from the pedantic job descriptions that Bud got HR to write they've got stuff like initiative, reliability, attendance, attitude, job knowledge, teamwork, productivity, judgement, innovation, responsiveness and participation'. The woman paused to breathe. It was just long enough for someone else to jump in.

'And what about presentation, leadership, enthusiasm and problem solving?' added another voice. 'The only thing they haven't got is form filling, and that's survival skill number one in this place.'

Bud had warned about the negative reaction from the team leaders, but it was the causes behind the frustrations that interested Santa and Georgie most. Breaking the group into four teams they asked the team leaders to discuss and identify what might be causing managers to focus on the hole instead of the donut and how that was affecting the performance review.

why focus on the hole?

After some lively discussions the teams rejoined as a full group to report back their thoughts.

Judging by the voices in support, the spokesperson for the first team seemed to have summed up the thoughts of everyone.

'To be honest, it's not just the managers who are negative. Everyone in the place is thinking that way and this list probably sums up why.'

Everyone looked at five points written in neat letters on a flip chart. The spokesperson briefly summed up what was on the sheet but the points, particularly the one about Bud, were crystal clear and logical.

Why we focus on the `hole'	Effect on the performance review
The company goals are unclear	Everyone has different views on what their goals should be
The review format is too detailed	It's easier to spot holes than things that are done well
The process is really bureaucratic	The boss runs the conversation
Bud says you don't praise someone for doing their job	You are expected to spot weaknesses when doing reviews or you're seen as a poor manager
The review is the only time that we give feedback	People get nasty surprises

'How does the performance review affect people afterwards? Do they just forget it or does it do some damage?' asked Santa.

Another team leader joined in. 'Well, that's the irony. The reviews take so much time to complete and the company must have spent millions on the computer system, yet it does more harm than good.'

'One of our best people resigned last month because of her performance review. She was an Administration Coordinator in the New Projects Office, which meant looking after up to six project managers at any time. She did a great job. No-one ever complained about her work. Then at the review her manager said she lacked initiative and couldn't follow instructions. She was furious. She'd been totally snowed under for the whole year and her boss never said a word about anything that needed improving. Straight after the review she just up and left, and now she's working for a competitor and we have to train a new person.'

'Does Ralph know about this?' asked Santa.

'Maybe,' replied someone, 'but he's got a grand ambition, so these days donuts are just something for him to eat at morning break'.

'What do you mean by "grand ambition"?' asked Georgie.

'Ralph has this crazy idea that he can buy up every company that is part of the Christmas value chain. He thinks he can own Christmas. The guy's dreaming. It's become such as obsession that he probably believes in Father Christmas.'

For the first time in her life Georgie was lost for words.

Time passed quickly on their first morning at Donut Delicacies, and Santa and Georgie found more than enough examples to help them understand the ills of the performance review. When they finished with the team leaders they spent a less than inspiring half hour with Bud who explained in great detail how the answer to curing the performance problems was an even more detailed performance review.

They looked forward to the next morning as they had been invited to attend a managers meeting chaired by the chief executive, Phil Sprinkler. Brad knew him personally and had arranged Santa and Georgie's attendance, much to the disgust of Bud, who told his ever-suffering personal assistant that he 'didn't like strangers butting in on company business'.

one way or two?

Santa and Georgie sat patiently in a room full of more than forty senior managers, some dressed in formal suits and others in the company shirt with the donut logo. The room had been arranged 'café style' with five separate tables, each accompanied by a flip chart. At the front a well-dressed woman was making last-minute adjustments to the focus of the data projector.

Phil Sprinkler opened the meeting by welcoming the visiting 'students' and thanked the managers for allocating a morning at short notice to consider an urgent issue.

Santa judged the Chief Executive to be in his forties, based on his receding blond hair greying at the tips and still-boyish face. He sensed a friendly person and the thought crossed his mind that there seemed a bit of a misfit between Bud and Phil.

From the briefing notes provided by Brad it seemed that Phil had spent most of the past eighteen months on matters outside the company due to funding issues that plagued most corporations following the global crisis. He was content to let his management team take care of the day-to-day issues, particularly as Ralph had built a strong business system and the company had done well in maintaining market share and revenue for the first twelve months. However, that had changed dramatically six months ago, prompting Phil to get a lot more hands-on.

Today was part of Phil's way of getting 'hands-on' and the managers were there to discuss and decide what action to take on a series of surveys that had been conducted across the organisation.

For ten minutes the Chief Executive showed the latest performance data. In a nutshell it painted a picture of a business off its game with declining revenue, increasing costs and dissatisfaction with its products and service from customers and retailers alike. No wonder Phil was coming under increasing pressure from XFS.

Handing over to the consultant, Tanja Perkovic, who had managed the survey administration and analysis, Phil walked past the tables where Santa and Georgie were sitting, gave them a knowing wink and sat down.

Tanja explained in a crisp, business-like tone that everyone had four sets of data in the folders in front of them.

Flicking on a slide divided into quadrants, she dispassionately, and a little bluntly in Santa's judgement, summarised the findings.

'Employee engagement has dropped dramatically in the past two quarters, particularly in Operations.' Bud's steel-capped boots shuffled and his ears reddened slightly. 'More than one-third of staff are considering alternative employment, and overall job satisfaction is the lowest ever recorded at Donut Delicacies.'

Tanja's style irritated Bud. Phil knew that. Phil wanted that.

It was a sentence of 'consultant speak' that finally pressed Bud's angry button. 'You will see that the 360-degree leadership feedback aligns almost perfectly with the engagement scores, which confirms what we know from our research, that manager behaviour is the strongest influence on employee engagement.'

Bud scoffed loudly enough for those at his table to notice. 'So why bother measuring both?' he asked smugly.

'You are the Head of Operations?' Tanja asked, putting Bud immediately on the defensive.

'Yeah', he replied more cautiously.

'Well, my advice, Mr Eldon, would be to look very closely at the 360-degree feedback for leaders of your division.'

She paused long enough to be sure that everyone in the room found and studied that page in their folders. They were looking at a train wreck.

'It's the lowest score in the company and you are right in a sense. With the data that low you don't have to do a survey to know that employees are not engaged.'

'They're not engaged because most of them are married, Miss', replied Bud sarcastically. A couple of Bud's cohorts laughed. Everyone else just cringed.

Tanja smiled. She'd met and dealt with plenty of bullies in her time.

'Can I be blunt?' she asked, walking slowly towards Bud until she was standing right in front of him.

'No, let me', interrupted Phil in a terse tone. He knew he didn't need to rescue Tanja from Bud. Quite the other way around.

'I direct this at everyone, but I suggest the Operations leaders hear me loud and clear. People are leaving this business due to bad management. Productivity is through the floor and that starts with poor management behaviour. We are here to find ways to fix bad management behaviour because the company can't afford not to.'

He turned to Tanja.'Please continue.'

The skilled facilitator quickly wrapped-up the summary and then allocated each table a specific question to answer. The first two tables were soon poring over the information and filling their flip chart with answers to the question,'Why is employee engagement falling?'

Santa's table and the one next to it were tackling,'Why is the performance review seen so negatively?'

Georgie's table had the question,'What skills are needed to make the performance review effective?'

She overheard someone explaining how his 'fail safe' strategy for getting a great review was to time a major achievement to the period just before the review.'You get the halo effect so your boss isn't game to give you anything but positive feedback', he advised.

Another agreed that it wasn't just about managers having skills because staff who were good at selling their accomplishments did better at reviews than those who just turned up and waited to be told by their manager.

A lively conversation on the merits of training staff in how to make the best use of the review and getting them more involved in the discussions ensued.

Just when the groups were finalising their 'top five' lists on the flip chart a table erupted in what sounded like a serious disagreement. Around the room conversations stopped and everyone listened.

'If you want to do a performance review properly, surely the manager also has to ask for feedback on his or her performance from the staff member. This has to be a two-way process', exhorted one manager.

Not surprisingly the other senior manager was Bud who, on realising that the room had quietened, stood and addressed the whole audience.

'The purpose of the performance review is for the manager to review the employee's performance. End of story. It's dangerous to have the employee evaluate the manager. They don't have the knowledge to do this. It will not happen in this company while Ralph Hampton Jr is the boss.'

'I run this company, not Ralph Hampton Jr', interjected the Chief Executive, joining a conversation that he had hoped would happen.

'Look at these flip charts', he said pointing firmly towards the outputs from the team activity. 'They're all telling us the same damn thing!' It was the first time the managers had seen Phil angry.

They looked at the posters and Phil was right. The answers were amazingly similar even though the questions were different.

Why is employee engagement falling?	Why is the performance review seen so negatively?
Too much focus on the hole and not the donut	Too much focus on the hole and not the donut
Lack of clear goals	Too detailed and bureaucratic
People get negative surprises at performance reviews	People get negative surprises
No feedback conversations between managers	The only source of feedback
Narrow and shallow conversations	Managers don't know how to conduct reviews properly
People don't trust their managers	Too infrequent

What is needed to make the performance review effective?

Focus on the donut, not the hole

Clearer company goals and values

Managers and staff with skills to have honest conversations

More-frequent feedback

A better, simpler system

Agreed purpose for the review

Phil continued. 'We've got disengaged people, low productivity, mistrust between managers and staff and increasing staff turnover. These are the classic effects of failed leadership and a malfunctioning performance system.'

'I take responsibility for the leadership failure', he said firmly. 'The economic crisis has been too easy an excuse for me to abdicate responsibility for setting the standards of leadership.'

Phil turned to Santa and Georgie. 'How do you think that we might fix the performance review?'

Bud was stunned. Consultants and now students. What next? He'd keep his mouth shut though. There were other ways to get around Mr Philip Sprinkler.

find the cause …

Georgie's mind was spinning at its usual rapid pace. The comment that the review focused on the hole instead of the donut seemed to describe so much that was wrong with the performance reviews at Santa Enterprises, Send Cards! and Donut Delicacies.

She asked Phil if she could use the whiteboard for a few minutes while everyone took a break. It was a popular decision as people dashed towards the waiting coffee and snacks.

Grabbing a bright orange pen Georgie went to work on the whiteboard. An idea was forming. After a burst of sketching, erasing and re-sketching she stood back and looked admiringly at her work.

'Hey, San, look at this.'

Santa looked at the whiteboard, surprised by how well Georgie could draw. In the top right corner was a perfectly drawn three-dimensional orange donut. In the hole were the words 'Fear of feedback'. In the top left corner was a strangely misshapen donut. In its off-centre hole was written 'Bureaucracy'. Santa laughed. It was what you'd expect when a bureaucracy made a donut. In the middle of the whiteboard was a half-chewed donut with the words 'Ill-equipped people' written in the hole. At the top of the whiteboard Georgie had written 'Why the review is ill'.

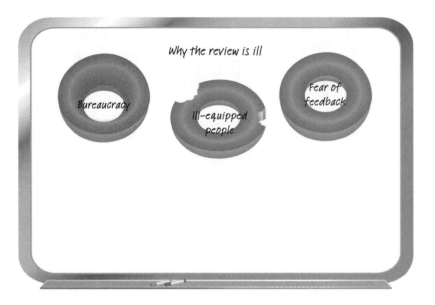

People wandered back into the room and soon there was a crowd around the whiteboard as Georgie explained how she had reduced all of the problems with the performance review (and possibly staff engagement) to three points.

Everyone took their seats and Phil challenged Georgie to test if all of the symptoms of the poor performance review fitted into just three areas.

'Well,' she said, enjoying the attention, 'if you call out all the things that you think are wrong with performance reviews, I'll see if they fit under these headings'.

It took less than ten minutes for Georgie to fill the space under the three donuts, and remarkably everything either fitted into one or more of the three categories, or was an effect of one of those symptoms. Even the employee engagement issues all fell into place.

Santa sat back, impressed by what Georgie had created. It was exactly what Brad had asked them to do—find the cause and you'll find the cure.

Even though the whiteboard contained a litany of problems with Donut Delicacies, Phil was pleased to have them out in the open as he rejoined Georgie at the front of the room.

'I understand from Brad that you and San will be doing some more travelling in search of the best way to cure the performance review', said Phil. They both nodded.

'We have to solve these problems to get this business back on track, so whatever you find you're most welcome to test your cure on us.'

Soon the room cleared leaving the two travellers to gather their thoughts before heading off to the airport.

'Hey, GM', said Georgie.

'Yes', replied Santa, wondering what was coming.

'How cool is this?' she said, grabbing a pen and writing on a notepad. 'We've got the framework for the cure.'

1 Simplify the bureaucratic process.

2 Equip people with the right attitude and skills.

3 Cure the fear of feedback.

Santa agreed. Their search for a cure was now much more focused. He was also pleased with Phil's invitation that they come back with a way to cure the review because Donut Delicacies seemed to have similar problems to those they were facing back at home.

have we found the root cause?

In previous chapters you assessed how performance reviews are conducted in your business. Before we move on to the exciting part of finding the cure, complete the following questionnaire to discover whether bureaucracy, ill-equipped people and fear of feedback are causing performance reviews to falter in your business.

questionnaire: are performance reviews faltering in your business?

Bureaucracy	Yes/No	Ill-equipped people	Yes/No	Fear of feedback	Yes/No
Too detailed	☐	Poorly pre-pared	☐	Avoidance of feedback	☐
Too time consuming	☐	Poor delivery of feedback	☐	Excuses, excuses	☐
Unclear or cross-purpose	☐	People give or get surprises	☐	Dumping or dancing	☐
Poor alignment to company goals	☐	Defensive	☐	Hiding behind status	☐
Doesn't suit the culture	☐	Staff don't know what to do	☐	No tough conversations	☐
Dumb ranking and rating	☐	Poor listening	☐	Narrow and shallow con-versations	☐
Encourages 'tick and flick'	☐	Handle emo-tions poorly	☐	One-way conversations	☐

Find the cause, find the cure.

part III

the prescription

chapter 8

true north

S ara Murchant, the Customer Service Manager for Santa Enterprises, had never seen so many complaints in all her years of service. She had also never known so many good people to leave the company.

Every year in mid January Sara would prepare a personal reply to any parent anywhere in the world who was unhappy with Santa's choice of toy for their child, or with the quality of the goods. This task usually took no more than two days because only a handful of people ever complained.

Today she scrolled a seemingly endless list of complaints on her computer screen: 'Same present as last year'; 'No batteries'; 'Why give a cricket bat to a girl in Russia?'; 'Did you mix up the naughty and nice list?'; 'Nice DVD but we don't have a player'; 'Our son doesn't like dolls'.

'How can I fix all these things when so many people in this company don't care about what they do anymore?' she wondered in dismay.

For a few minutes she just sat, overwhelmed. Even the diligent and loyal Sara didn't have the energy to begin the horrible task of replying one by one to the thousands of people who had complained.

'I'll go for a hike to the summit', she thought. 'The cold air always clears my mind.'

A few minutes later, after pulling on her sturdiest hiking boots and placing some fruit in a small red duffle bag, the fit, wiry Customer Service Manager was steadily climbing the steepest of the pathways that led south from the village towards a rocky, snow-covered summit, which was the highest point in the nearby hills.

It took just under thirty minutes to reach the narrow track of snow and broken rocks that led the final 100 metres to the summit.

Clambering between the final two boulders Sara was startled to find another person already sitting on the large, flat circular rock that provided the perfect and only place on the otherwise jagged summit to sit and enjoy the view.

Brad was equally surprised to see his Customer Service Manager.

'What brings you up here?' she asked, getting in first and hoping that he wouldn't ask the same question.

'Oh, I needed to do some thinking and this seemed the perfect place.'

Brad could see that Sara was uncomfortable and made small talk about whether they could see the North Pole from there and how beautiful the misty valley looked in the afternoon light.

Then they sat in silence, buffeted occasionally by gusts of chilly wind and their own thoughts.

Sara was not one to share her worries with others and certainly not with the Chief Executive. She would take the long winding trail back across the ridges. That would give her time to think.

Brad needed something different. He liked to bounce ideas off people, so the arrival of Sara on the craggy peak was perfect timing.

She stood to escape. 'Sara, before you go, can I ask your opinion on something?'

She shuffled and nodded while he remained seated.

'What can I do to improve this company?'

'That was it?' she thought with some panic. 'He wants me to tell him how to run the company?'

'I think you're doing a fine job', she replied in an all-too-obvious attempt to escape the conversation.

Brad smiled. 'Thank you.'

He stood and faced the Customer Service Manager who was now bobbing from one foot to another as if seeking just the right moment to sprint away down the track.

'Sara, you are weighed down with customer complaints, and it's hard to imagine that morale could get any lower, so there must be some feedback that you can give me.' He then added one word that made all the difference: 'Please?'

Three hours later the Chief Executive and the Customer Service Manager shook hands at the junction where the long summit track met the main valley track. Both felt like a load had lifted from their shoulders.

Sara had never given feedback to a chief executive before. In fact, she never gave feedback to anyone other than her team, and then it was only encouragement. If something needed fixing, she usually did it herself or waited to see if things would right themselves. Perhaps it was a reason her team seemed dissatisfied and she was so overwhelmed with work. That thought had never crossed her mind before.

Brad knew that chief executives could command most things—resources, attention, power, money and opportunity—but the hardest of all to get was feedback. People just would not give feedback to their bosses, and when you are the boss of bosses, well, it is almost mission impossible.

Through skilful questioning Brad had helped Sara give him the feedback he craved. Without her open and honest comments he wouldn't have seen what was missing in his leadership and in the business. In doing so he had also helped Sara realise that feedback wasn't something to fear, and when the chief executive suggested that she could be a better leader by sharing her problems with colleagues and staff, it seemed reassuring, not threatening.

clear and compelling

Back in his office Brad jotted down what he had gleaned from the conversation.

> We need everyone to be able to answer the four big questions for their team and their job:
>
> • Why are we here?
> • What must we achieve?
> • How will we achieve those things?
> • What values and principles will guide us?

With the incessant and not unreasonable badgering from XFS about cash flow he'd been too preoccupied looking at the day-to-day problems to realise the most fundamental thing. People didn't know where the company was heading or how they could make a positive contribution.

Santa Enterprises didn't have a clear and compelling Why, What and How, and because of that every department, every team and every individual had a different view of why they were there and what was important.

Sure, the long-serving staff shared a common set of values, but the acquisition and turnover meant that there was no longer what he used to call a 'True North' to give people that sense of direction. And how appropriate that term seemed in this place so close the North Pole.

It was so obvious. He would set up a video conference with Georgie and Santa immediately. 'It's no wonder the performance review isn't working!' he thought, feeling almost silly for not seeing it before. How could it without a True North?

---

have you done 'values 101'?

Almost every company and government agency has a list of values on its website and hanging behind the reception desk. However, it is only those companies that take the time and effort to embed the values in the systems and behaviours of the business that are rewarded with greater engagement of staff, more satisfied customers, better partners and higher returns for shareholders.

Sure, 'values 101' sounds like a university course, but it is the foundation for strategic plans, performance reviews and all other performance systems. It is how you go from a nice set of words to a living part of the business culture.

Take the values 101 test by reading the following details, and then completing the self-reflection questionnaire.

have you done 'values 101'? *(cont'd)*

→ *People know what the values mean.* You can ask anyone in the business what a value means and they get it: immediately, logically and emotionally. Take 'integrity', for example. If people tell you it's just about being honest, they don't get it. On the other hand, if they talk about doing the right thing by all the values, having a standard or code of ethics, or acting with integrity of character, you know they do get it.

→ *People live the values twenty-four seven.* You can't switch your core values on and off. If you can, they're not values and are likely to disappear when the pressure is on. It goes without saying that you either live the values in your behaviour or you don't. People such as Ted and HR Harry will argue passionately that they live the values. Let others judge whether you do or don't—and ask for that view.

→ *The values are a guide to decision making.* The best sign that values are getting into the 'DNA' of the business is when a team uses the values to either shape or test their decisions. For example, think about how you would deal with someone such as Bud Eldon if you were the chief executive of Donut Delicacies. The temptation might be to march those steel-capped boots straight out the front door, but what do the business values tell you? If those values are about integrity, teamwork and performance, they give you a guide as to how best to handle Bud.

→ *Leaders promote and instil the values.* When values are an integral part of the business the leaders at all levels play a part in promoting their practical use. This means making them meaningful as a set of guidelines that people use in their decision making and to guide their behaviour. Good leaders can use values in a room full of cynics and make them powerful, not an academic, 'feel-good' exercise.

→ *Challenging breaches of the values.* This is the hardest thing to do because not only do people avoid giving feedback (particularly about behaviour), but they are usually ill-equipped to do so.

How do you personally fare on the values 101 test? Take a few moments to complete the following questionnaire.

---

questionnaire: self-reflection

	Never	Rarely	Some-times	Often	Al-ways
1 I live the values twenty-four seven.	☐	☐	☐	☐	☐
2 I use the values to guide my decision making.	☐	☐	☐	☐	☐
3 I promote and rein-force the values.	☐	☐	☐	☐	☐
4 I challenge breaches.	☐	☐	☐	☐	☐

Any ticks below 'Always' suggest that you are ready to lay the foundation for curing the performance review.

---

finding true north

It is amazing how few businesses have a simple process for defining the *Why*, *What* and *How* at each level of the organisation. They all have detailed strategic and business plans, but ask for a simple one-page explanation that answers Brad's first three questions (Why are we here? What must we achieve? How will we achieve those things?) and you typically get some blank looks.

finding true north *(cont'd)*

The absence of direction, of this True North, makes it almost impossible for managers and team leaders to get the essential align-ment from company priorities and goals, back through department goals, then team goals and finally into individual goals and objectives. If that is the case, the performance management cycle is doomed to failure. The lack of an integrated True North also fosters silo behaviour because it allows and encourages departments to do their own priority setting in isolation.

Complete the following questionnaire to find out if your business has a True North.

questionnaire: does your business have a True North?

	Whole of business	Department	Individual
Why are we here? (A simple statement that describes purpose)	Yes/No	Yes/No	Yes/No
What must we achieve? (The top five priorities)	Yes/No	Yes/No	Yes/No
How will we achieve those things? (Key actions to achieve the priorities)	Yes/No	Yes/No	Yes/No

If your answers to the questionnaire include any 'No' responses then there is some work to be done to create the alignment of goals that sets the foundation for performance conversations.

Without alignment to True North the review is set up to fail.

chapter 9

feedback expectation

After a long flight across the Pacific, Santa and Georgie got out of their taxi at yet another hotel, this time on the island of Singapore.

It took only the five or so steps from the car to air-conditioned foyer for Santa to break out into a sweat in the steamy tropical heat. Fortunately, unlike previous stops this one was for rest and recovery. He looked forward to a few quiet moments to himself, starting with a nice after-noon nap as soon as he had completed the check-in, which he would if he could find that impish woman and get her to sign for her room.

Never one to let a moment pass without doing some-thing, Georgie had spotted a colourful display of tourist brochures in the hotel foyer. Santa groaned when he saw her flicking through them.

'Hey, San', she called across the marble foyer. 'How about we go on the big observation wheel, the Singapore Flyer, then go on a water slide and maybe a game of golf?'

'No, no and no', replied the weary Santa with unusual sternness.

Georgie was hurt, and made sure that he noticed as she rejoined him to sign for her room.

'Georgie, I need some rest, so maybe we could just hit golf balls later at the driving range?' he suggested as something of a peace offering.

The concierge who had been hovering waiting for a tip stepped forward. 'Sir, as we are part of the Country Club I can arrange golf for you at 5.00 pm. Would you like a lesson with our resident professional?' he asked. 'He's a very good coach.'

'Super', came the reply from Georgie before Santa could even think.

'Okay', he agreed reluctantly, which was the signal for the bellboy to wheel his suitcases towards the elevator that he hoped would deliver him to a cool, quiet and dark room well away from Georgie.

golf, anyone?

It was one minute to 5.00 pm and Georgie was knocking excitedly on Santa's door.

'All right, all right', he called, still half asleep and struggling towards the door.

'You go ahead and get started. I'll join you in a few minutes when I've woken properly.'

Georgie was already well into her lesson with Mr Peng, the golf professional, when Santa arrived wearing long white socks, bermuda shorts and a crisply ironed red polo shirt. Georgie whistled her approval, which did nothing to settle the great man who had never hit a golf ball in his life and until today hadn't planned to either.

Mr Peng, a short, well-muscled Singaporean of Chinese descent, walked over to shake hands with Santa leaving Georgie happily and quite skilfully hitting balls from the carpet mat onto a field that was almost covered in white golf balls.

'What do you hope to achieve from this golf lesson?' Mr Peng asked in a manner that gave Santa some confidence that this wasn't going to be the most embarrassing hour of his life.

'I don't play golf', stammered Santa, 'so I guess it would be nice to learn the basics'.

Mr Peng nodded reassuringly. 'Of course, and do you have any other expectations for this lesson?'

'Just that you are patient with me because this is something totally new.'

Mr Peng smiled. 'Of course, Mr San. If you work with me in partnership, we can learn together and help you to become a very good golfer.'

Santa laughed at the idea of becoming a good golfer.

His coach continued. 'I suggest that our goal today is that you are able to hit a ball at least 100 metres by the end of our lesson and that you enjoy this time and learn some love for the game of golf.'

Mr Peng made his student feel very comfortable. Santa thought he was indeed a very good coach and happily agreed to a final request that they were both open and honest in their conversations with each other during the lesson.

Moving to the driving range the coach guided him through a series of warm-up exercises, which Santa felt to be unnecessary in the heat but the experienced golf coach assured him that it would help with rhythm and timing, neither of which he expected to achieve. While doing the stretches the great man explained how he and Georgie were on a mission to cure the ills of the performance review, but that the visit to Singapore was just for recovery before flying on to Australia.

Over the next thirty minutes Mr Peng divided his time between Georgie, who needed to be reminded about concentration, and Santa, who had mastered the grip and was starting to hit balls consistently in the air with a seven iron.

'Head still and slow takeaway', advised Mr Peng. 'How did that feel?'

'Quite easy, actually', replied Santa.

'Excellent, just keep that pace and rhythm in your swing and remember to hit down through the ball.'

Santa was enjoying the golf until Mr Peng advised that he would be gone for ten minutes and disappeared into his office at the back of the driving range. Unfortunately Mr Peng's disappearance also coincided with Georgie becoming bored with hitting balls. She decided that the man in the bermuda shorts would benefit from her advice.

'A bit more turn of the shoulder, GM', she advised as his club dug hard into the green carpet sending the ball just a few feet to his right and jarring his left wrist. 'Oh, and not so quick on the back swing.'

Santa glowed red. He was frustrated and annoyed. He didn't want Georgie coaching him.

'Where's that Mr Peng?' he thought. 'I'm paying for him to coach me, not this annoying woman who doesn't know any more than I do!'

removing the obstacles to feedback conversations

Mr Peng had been watching from his office and chose that moment to rejoin them. 'Did you notice anything when I wasn't with you for the past ten minutes?'

'Yes,' replied the still-agitated Santa, 'my colleague started to coach me and, with respect, that wasn't very helpful'.

'Of course, Georgie was trying to be most helpful', said Mr Peng. Georgie wasn't quite sure whether to be complimented or insulted.

'And what did you expect from me as your coach?'

'I expected you to be here and to help me to improve.'

'Yes, you quite reasonably expected that we would work in partnership and I apologise for leaving you. But before you try for the goal of hitting a ball 100 metres are there lessons here that you might apply to your search for the cure to the performance review?'

Santa and Georgie looked at each other.

'Are there?' they asked in unison.

Mr Peng had spent his whole life giving and receiving feedback, and he could never understand why so many businesspeople seemed fearful of giving others feedback. This seemed like a good opportunity to pass on some of his skills and experiences to help his guests in their mission to cure the review. In fact, what he had to say was going to be a major breakthrough for Georgie and Santa.

'Here today you have seen the complete opposite of what happens in the business workplace.'

'In what way?' asked Santa.

'Well, San, I believe that you and I agreed to work in partnership to improve your golf game, and we set a goal and some other expectations. And we agreed to give open and honest feedback to each other so that you could make those improvements and enjoy the game.'

Mr Peng motioned them over to a whiteboard that was fastened to the back wall of the driving range. He wrote the words 'Feedback expectation' on the whiteboard and turned to his guests. 'The expectation was of a partnership, with feedback being given often. You expected feedback and even became annoyed when you didn't get it.'

Santa was beginning to realise how different things were when you actually wanted and expected feedback. Mr Peng continued.

'Have you noticed in your travels that most businesses do not create this feedback expectation, so either people don't get any feedback at all, which means more errors and slower learning, or when it does come it is like Georgie's coaching. Unwelcome.'

Georgie wasn't sure if Mr Peng was taking the micky out of her, but for her colleague the light was coming on.

'You're absolutely right!' Santa exclaimed with more energy than Georgie had seen in a long time.'It's no wonder people fear feedback in the workplace and are scared of the review. We don't properly set up the expectation that feedback happens all the time. We set up an expectation that feedback happens at the six- or twelve-monthly review, which means you don't know what's coming.'

'And that feedback, if it is even relevant, is too late and one way', added Mr Peng.

Georgie jumped in. 'Mr Peng, you used the word partnership. Why is that so important?'

It was the question he had hoped she would ask. 'My success as a coach can only come from the golfer. But I cannot help the golfer if we can't work in partnership, which means agreeing to a common goal, some expectations about behaviour and a level of trust so we can be open and honest with our feedback.'

They could see a link but it required just one more piece of advice from the Singaporean golf coach.

'If you want to cure this fear of feedback that business people have, then create a strong partnership between the manager and direct report, and between colleagues. That partnership is what you might call a "feedback relationship" because both partners want and expect feedback from each other. Just imagine how different your workplace would be if you eliminated the fear of feedback and had these feedback partnerships.'

A large light globe had just gone on for Santa, but something still troubled Georgie. 'When I tried to give San feedback, why didn't that work? Aren't we partners?' she asked with a hint of disappointment.

'Because there are natural obstacles to giving and receiving feedback, and you didn't create the feedback expectation that removes many of those obstacles.'

Mr Peng could see that she was still a little unsure and needed one of his favourite tools to help her. 'I always remember it this way', he commented while scribbling three letters down the side of the whiteboard and then filling in the details. 'If I want to create a feedback expectation with a partner, then I 'GET' these three things in place.'

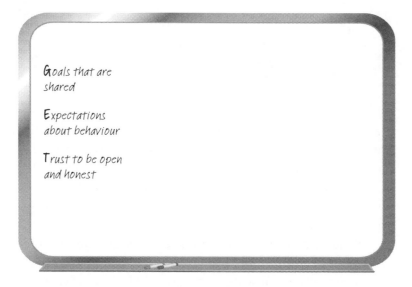

Goals that are
shared

Expectations
about behaviour

Trust to be open
and honest

'Sounds like Brad's True North', thought Georgie, looking at 'Goals that are shared' and reflecting on the most recent video conference with their boss.

It was so obvious. Mr Peng had made sure there was a feedback expectation between himself and Santa (which fostered a partnership), but there was no such expectation between Santa and Georgie. Finally, they filled in the whiteboard with those details.

	Coaching by Mr Peng	Coaching by Georgie
Goals that are shared	• Hit balls 100 metres	• No goals agreed
Expectations about behaviour	• Partnership • We will share feedback • We will be open and honest	• No expectations agreed • Implicit expectation is 'no feedback'
Trust to be open and honest	• Yes	• No
	Effect Feedback expectation	*Effect* Feedback avoidance

'If you don't lay the groundwork to *GET* a feedback expectation with employees and colleagues, your performance review is doomed to failure because people have no basis for having open and honest conversations about behaviour. It's a paradox that if you really do create the feedback expectation, you might discover that the traditional performance review is not needed.'

Santa and Georgie would think a lot more about this in the coming days.

'Now, let's hit those balls', suggested Mr Peng, interrupting their thoughts.

Handing Santa a six iron he asked him what the three or four key cues of his swing were.

'Head still, low take away. Hit down through the ball and follow through', announced the now-confident golfer.

Georgie held her breath as the jolly man took a practice swing and then settled into his stance. She had nothing to worry about as after a couple of wiggles he not only hit one ball past the 100 metre flag, but hit three in a row.

A simple golf lesson in Singapore would change forever the way a company in Lapland thought about open and honest conversations and performance reviews.

the prescription

When they returned to their hotel they began to construct a framework for what Georgie called 'the Prescription', and while it had plenty of holes, it was starting to fill.

The prescription		
For bureaucracy: align	For ill-equipped people: equip	For fear of feedback: partner
True North		Feedback Expectation

creating the feedback expectation

Is it really a breakthrough idea to suggest that creating a feedback expectation is fundamental to having open and honest conversations? Amazingly, this seems to be the case. Most of the organisations I have worked with found significant improvements just from implementing

creating the feedback expectation *(cont'd)*

the GET part of the framework. It seems that this is a key element in creating the partnership that Mr Peng spoke about and, ultimately, to eliminating the fear of feedback.

G is for goals — make them SMARTA

A large percentage of the so-called goals or objectives that are recorded in personal performance plans are little more than vague statements of intention. This is despite the thousands of books written on goal setting and the insistence of people that they are skilled at goal setting.

The best way to set effective goals is to apply the SMARTA test. A common goal chosen by people is to 'get fit and healthy'. As much as this is a good intention, it is not a goal and you can see why by completing the following questionnaire.

Choose one of your current work or personal goals and test it against the SMARTA criteria.

---

questionnaire: are your goals SMARTA?

	Not at all	Some-what	Definitely
Specific — you know exactly what it means	☐	☐	☐
Measurable — you can measure whether it has been achieved or not	☐	☐	☐
Achievable — it is realistic but challenging	☐	☐	☐
Relevant — it fits with your higher purpose or vision	☐	☐	☐
Timed — it has a completion date	☐	☐	☐
Agreed — your key partners support this	☐	☐	☐

E is for expectations — confirmed early and reviewed often

Business (and personal) relationships all have significant expectations attached to them, so it is not surprising that creating a partnership where both parties feel comfortable enough to give and receive feedback requires a conversation about expectations. (Georgie found out what happens when you give feedback and there is no expectation.) Those expectations fall into two broad categories:

→ deliverables — outputs and outcomes that people expect of us and we of them

→ behaviours — behaviours that people do or do not display.

One of the keys to effective and sustainable partnering is to establish and then meet each others' expectations. Ideally, those expectations are established in the framework of a True North for the business, for teams and for individuals.

T is for trust — the foundation for performance conversations

What comes first? Trust or the open conversation?

Few things build trust better than sharing open and honest feedback with each other. The challenge, however, is that we rarely have those types of conversations until we establish trust.

Trust is a complex topic that requires more detail and coaching, but the model overleaf is a helpful starting point for you to build trust with colleagues, staff and managers. Use it to reflect on your business relationships and to consider if people with whom you hold performance conversations would view you as approachable, open, dependable and of high integrity.

The starting point for strengthening any of these four elements is self-awareness. Perhaps a colleague or coach can help you to build this awareness and to strengthen any areas of concern.

creating the feedback expectation *(cont'd)*

Approachable	Open
People need to feel that having a conversation with you is a safe thing to do and that you will treat them as an equal.	People will be open if they see you being open in expressing your thoughts and feelings, and being open to their ideas and feedback.
Dependable	**Integrity**
People will be more likely to trust you when they know they can rely on you to be competent and to do what you say you will do.	People will judge you to have integrity if they view you as being ethical and of trustworthy character.

Is it time for you to GET a feedback expectation with your direct reports and/or manager?

feedback culture — not a review culture

Sydney, Australia. About as far away from Lapland as you can get.

'Business travel is seriously hard work', moaned Georgie after the overnight flight from Singapore.

It was an hour since they landed and they were still nowhere near the front of the snaking queue of tired travellers that was inching its way towards the customs inspection. Another hour passed before they finally arrived at their hotel on the esplanade of Bondi Beach, but it must have been their day for delays because their rooms were not available until 3.00 pm.

'It's the system', explained the polite receptionist.

'Why can't they make systems that work for people?' muttered Santa as he and Georgie took the offer to change clothes and head to the beach.

'You'd better get some sunscreen or you'll be looking like Rudolph in no time', chirped Georgie soon after they laid towels on the golden sand.

'This one's for Mrs Claus', she giggled, snapping a photo on her phone of the jolly fellow sprawled on an Australian beach with zinc cream on his nose and an already threatening red glow across the rest of his marble white body.

'Don't you dare!' he demanded, lunging for the phone.

The great man wondered what Mrs Claus would say and how it would feel to be sunburned. By 10.00 that night he knew the answer to both questions and they involved heat, discomfort and the need for a quick remedy.

invite, accept and offer

At nine the next morning Santa and Georgie were greeted by two executives of O'Donnell's Jelly Bean Company, makers of the world's best jelly beans and a company they had chosen to visit because of its reputation for being at the leading edge of human resource practices.

'What have you discovered on your study tour?' enquired the pleasant and professional Chief Executive, Jenny O'Donnell, daughter of one of company's founders.

'Well, I'm afraid that most businesses invest a lot of time and effort in performance reviews, but get more trouble than value from them', replied Santa.

'Yeah', nodded Steve Edwards, Head of Operations. 'They tend to be as user-unfriendly as possible.'

'Like getting through an airport', commented Georgie to everyone's agreement.

'How can we help you?' asked Jenny.

Santa explained that they had identified the three root causes of the ills of the review—bureaucracy, ill-equipped people and fear of feedback—and that they were now seeking cures.

'I'm not sure if we're going to be much help to you', explained Jenny. 'We decided to get rid of the formal performance review and replace it with just two items.'

'Really?' Santa asked taken aback. 'What are those two items?'

'Giving honest feedback to colleagues and being open to accepting feedback from colleagues.'

'That's it?' Georgie exclaimed rather too loudly.

Steve and Jenny smiled, appreciating her energy and enthusiasm. Santa winced at his colleague's bluntness, and that made his shirt rub against his tender sunburned shoulders.

'Why did you get rid of the review and replace it with just those two?' asked Santa.

'It's quite simple', chipped in Steve. 'The review had become so bureaucratic and tired that it was preventing people being honest with each other. In this tough economic climate we needed a feedback culture, not a review culture, so we dropped the review.'

Steve could see that they didn't really understand what he meant, so he went on. 'We assumed for years that the review was essential to the whole feedback loop between managers and their direct reports, but when we looked at it closely we got the proverbial lightning bolt.'

'Which was?' asked Santa.

'Performance reviews and feedback are at cross-purposes. For example, in my operations group the supervisors were waiting for the review to give feedback instead of making feedback a regular part of work. The feedback was too late, which was causing quality and morale problems, and people hated reviews because they got nasty surprises about things that happened months earlier.'

'And staff weren't giving honest feedback to their managers or colleagues,' added Jenny, 'because they feared the review and its consequences for things like pay rises and promotions. They waited for the 360-degree survey that was supposed to be about development, not regular feedback. Every way you looked at it the performance review was a big obstacle to open, honest performance conversations, and that was costing us money'.

'I see', said Georgie, 'so if you can get people to give and receive honest feedback all the time, then the performance review becomes irrelevant because when it comes around the conversations have already happened and there's nothing to review. Cool!'

'Exactly!' replied Jenny, smiling.

'But how do you get past the fear of feedback and the lack of skills?' asked Georgie thinking about her three donuts.

'That's not easy and there's no one simple answer', replied Steve. 'But we started by testing a program called Everyone Coaches, and that's made a big difference to giving people the skills and confidence to make performance conversations a part of everyday work.'

'What does it involve?' asked Santa, who was intrigued by the name Everyone Coaches, particularly after their experience with Mr Peng in Singapore.

'You'll see during the day because we've arranged for you to join the Sales and Marketing team, which is doing the first two stages of the program', replied Jenny. 'Basically it's about learning how to invite, accept and offer effective feedback. And that's what good coaches do—every day.'

'Let's meet up later for dinner to hear all about your day. Hopefully you can offer some suggestions on how we can improve this further', said Steve, as he led them through the factory that produced the brightly coloured giant jelly beans for which O'Donnell's was world famous. It was going to be a day of surprises for the two travellers.

do you *want* feedback?

The twenty-five members of the Sales and Marketing team were seated in a spacious and bright training room chatting among themselves as they waited for the facilitator, Bec Arthur, to open proceedings.

After a brief comment from Jimmy Chew, the Head of Sales and Marketing, Bec introduced herself to those who didn't know her and explained that the purpose of the day was to learn coaching skills and to practise inviting, accepting and offering feedback.

She then asked everyone to introduce themselves and to share two words that described their current feelings. Words such as *scared, nervous* and *uncomfortable* made Santa realise that this was no ordinary training session, but *excited, hopeful* and *ready* suggested that they were looking forward to getting out of their comfort zones. Georgie's contribution of *pumped* and *zoned* eluded him.

After everyone had introduced themselves Bec began in her friendly and open style. 'Our goal at O'Donnell's is to make the best jelly beans in the world.' She paused while a number of people nodded, and then fired a question at the group, catching quite a few unawares.

'So how can we do that when there are competitors everywhere and the economy is still recovering from the financial crisis?'

There was silence. Bec waited. Finally someone spoke.

'You've gotta keep getting better', Georgie advised with her customary frankness.

'Is she right?' asked the facilitator of a graphic designer from advertising.

'Yes.'

'Why?' she pressed, not content to just let people be spectators.

'Because the only way to be the best is to stay ahead of the rest.'

Everyone laughed at exactly the response you'd expect from someone in advertising.

'How do *you* keep getting better?' the facilitator enquired of a woman whose permed hair, three-string pearls and circa 1980s business suit seemed out of place among the casually stylish marketing team.

'Relentless improvement', she replied dismissively.

Bec wanted more. 'And how do you get relentless improvement?' she asked of the woman, who Georgie had decided would be known as 'the Queen'.

'By getting feedback and then using it to improve', replied the Queen in a tone that hinted trouble, but the experienced facilitator moved on, knowing that her ladyship was in for an interesting day.

Stepping back from the group Bec pointed to posters placed around the room. Starting from her right was a poster with the words *Totally agree* on it in large bold letters. The next poster along the wall was *Agree*, facing her on the back wall was *Disagree*, and then along the wall to her left were *Totally disagree* and *Don't know*.

'Consider this statement and then move to the poster that best describes your view: "I want more feedback from colleagues so I can grow and develop".'

Everyone moved close to *Totally agree*, although the Queen was noticeably slow to arrive.

'What does this mean?' Bec asked of the group with a laugh.

Several people replied and each made pretty much the same point.

'We all want feedback, provided that it is constructive and given at the right time.'

'And when is the right time?'

'As soon as possible but probably not in front of others if it's something that needs correcting', replied Tracey from Sales.

'Why not in public?' asked Bec.

'I guess none of us likes to be made to look bad in front of others.'

'Don't sportspeople get feedback in front of their teams all the time?' asked Georgie.

'Good point', replied Tracey. 'But they expect it.'

'Why don't you expect it?' pushed Georgie.

'Because it's not part of the culture', replied Tracey.

'Not yet', suggested Bec. 'And …'

'And it's not necessary', interrupted the Queen. 'That is what the performance review is for.'

Bec smiled to herself. Georgie imagined how the Queen used the performance review as a weapon of mass humiliation. Others imagined how nice it would be if she'd resign.

'Next statement', announced the facilitator. 'I don't like giving open and honest critical feedback to my colleagues, direct reports and boss.'

There was a small stampede towards the *Totally agree* and *Agree* posters. Only Tracey, Dominic the New Products Manager and the Queen stood on the other side of the room.

The group discussed why people don't give feedback and Bec put the reasons on a flip chart.

Why people don't give feedback

Don't want to upset people

Not my job to do that

Wait until performance review

Not good at giving feedback

Don't like creating conflict

The other person won't listen anyway

Might damage the relationship

Even Tracey and Dominic conceded that they found it difficult to give unsolicited critical feedback. The Queen, who seemed bored by the activity, advised with extraordinary certainty that in her experience giving feedback to staff was simple and necessary, but to give it to colleagues and your manager was inappropriate.

'Fear of feedback', thought Santa. 'Ill-equipped people', thought Georgie. 'Pompous old bag', thought everyone else.

'Look at these,' said Bec motioning to the flip chart. 'You all want feedback, but the very people who you want and need it from aren't able or willing to give it to you.'

'So what is the answer, dear?' asked the Queen.

'Pull feedback', said Bec a touch too bluntly, and quickly realising her need to explain, continued, 'Business systems such as the performance review are based on the premise that people are given feedback by their superiors. Our model turns that upside down and puts the responsibility on you to invite or pull feedback from everyone'.

The Queen sniffed. She was becoming increasingly concerned with where this young facilitator was leading them. She would (unsuccessfully) discuss this with Jimmy during the break that Bec had just called.

feedback drought

The Sales and Marketing team returned to a room that was completely different from the one they had left just a few minutes earlier. The tables were pushed back against the walls creating a large open space, and the chairs were in a semi-circle, while posters with the phrases *Feedback relationship, Debrief–Learn–Adapt, REAL and RITE,* and *Invite feedback* hung on the walls

Of most interest to the participants was a table at the front of the room that was littered with bright orange yoyos.

Bec reminded everyone that the purpose of the day was to give them the skills to constructively invite, accept and offer feedback.

Flicking on a PowerPoint slide with the words *What's your attitude to critical feedback?* on it in large letters, she explained. 'A big obstacle to us inviting the truth is the attitude or the beliefs that we have about critical feedback.'

In their Everyone Coaches workbooks a questionnaire with situations and a rating scale enabled everyone to reflect on their personal attitudes to receiving critical feedback. In small groups people discussed the situations, shared why some were more difficult than others and searched for patterns to explain their reaction.

Bec asked what would help them to be more comfortable with handling critical feedback. One small group used the whiteboard to discuss three different types of critical feedback.

Feedback	Characterised by
Valid	Justified, accurate, reasonable, factual comments
Invalid	Unjustified, inaccurate, biased comments
Fuzzy	Unclear and personal comments, opinion instead of facts

'Should we react the same way to all types of critical feedback?' called out Bec.

Some, mostly the males plus the Queen, were adamant that invalid criticism must be tackled head on. Others, mostly females, pointed out that defensiveness will shut down the feedback even if the criticism is unfair.

There would be time later for Bec to point out how males tend to look for things outside themselves as causes of criticism while females tend to look inwards.

'Let's test this out', she suggested, pulling up a chair and sitting in the middle of the room. 'Give me some valid, critical feedback on how I'm facilitating this workshop.'

Silence.

'This proves that people don't like giving feedback, doesn't it', she laughed.

From her left came a young voice. 'I don't think you're giving us enough instruction.' It was Hamish, a new graduate in marketing and communications and the youngest person in the room.

'That's not valid', jumped in one of the sales team. 'Yeah, it's not fair', said another, eager to defend the facilitator.

Hamish shrank back in his chair.

'Let's look at what's happening here', said Bec. 'The feedback has been rejected before it even got to me! Hamish, are you going to give me any more feedback today?'

'No', he replied sheepishly.

Bec wrote on the whiteboard.

> ## To _discourage_ people from giving you feedback:
>
> React ☒ Resist ☒ Reject

'The attitude you show towards feedback is so important', she stressed. 'If you aggressively defend like we just saw, or even just more passively ignore it, the effect is the same—a feedback drought.'

open for feedback

The facilitator wanted to push the group a little further. 'Find me a better model that tells people that you are open for the truth.'

Everyone went to work in small groups and a few minutes later a new version emerged from a full group discussion, which Bec again wrote on the whiteboard:

> ## To <u>discourage</u> people from giving you feedback:
>
> React ⟶ Resist ⟶ Reject
>
> ## To <u>encourage</u> people to give you feedback:
>
> Receive ⟶ Reflect ⟶ Respond

'Excellent. And so simple. I "receive" by thanking Hamish for his feedback but not react immediately. Ask for time to "reflect" and pop in a few questions to better understand his views.'

'What about "respond"?' queried Hamish, again feeling a part of the workshop.

'It's up to me to choose how I want to respond to your feedback, but the main point is that you continue to be willing to give me feedback.'

'Are you going to respond?' asked Georgie.

'Yes, I am, because thanks to Hamish's feedback I know that at least one person wasn't sure where the session was heading or why I was insisting that you find your own answers to some of these issues. I'll be more aware of explaining the *why* behind *what* we are doing.

'Thanks, Hamish', she said, flashing an encouraging smile in his direction.

Bec picked up one of the bright orange yoyos, put the loop at the end of the string on her middle finger and with a flick of the wrist propelled it towards the floor, where it stopped and spun rapidly. Quickly gathering up string one section at time she soon had the spinning yoyo swinging like a pendulum.

'Rocking the cradle', she announced, still concentrating on the yoyo. 'Some of you will recognise it.' The older members of the group nodded, recalling their childhoods. The Queen muttered something about wasting valuable time on children's games.

Bec let the yoyo drop, and then just before it hit the floor jerked quickly on the swing, causing it to flick up-wards and spin back into her hand to a generous round of applause.

'Okay, let's be clear', announced the facilitator. 'There are two goals here. The first is to learn enough about yoyos to be able to coach someone and the second is to get up to speed fast on coaching tools to give reinforcement and critical feedback.'

For the next thirty minutes the coaching went smoothly until Georgie decided that she was ready for an advanced skill called slingshot. In her first and only attempt she gave Jimmy Chew a fearsome crack on the back of the head with her orange yoyo.

After some brisk head rubbing and much apologising all was forgiven, and soon everyone, even the Queen, had mastered the basics and was having fun.

direct, specific behaviour-changing feedback

Bec was pleased to see the yoyos in action, but the business reason they were there was to learn a technique to give direct, specific behaviour-changing feedback. She invited the group to give feedback on her coaching.

'Great', 'Good', Excellent', 'Fine', came the first replies.

'With respect, that's not feedback', she said to a few surprised looks. 'That's just encouragement. What exactly do you want to reinforce so I keep doing it?'

The reinforcements flowed from the group as soon as people thought about being direct and specific: 'The simple instructions', 'Making it okay to make mistakes', 'Demonstrating things in small steps', 'Giving one-on-one coaching'.

They understood a fundamental principle of coaching: be specific in your reinforcement.

be REAL

Bec asked Dominic, the New Products Manager, to try rocking the cradle and to invite, or 'pull', feedback from the group. 'Make the feedback specific — and let's start with reinforcements to build Dominic's confidence', she instructed.

Everyone watched as he methodically set up the rhythm of flicking the yoyo up and down, and then made a pretty good attempt at rocking the cradle.

He then asked his colleagues, 'Is there any feedback that you can offer me?'

The Queen couldn't help herself. 'You're not very good at flicking the yoyo, and the cradle was uneven.'

There was an audible groan around the room. It was obvious to everyone, except the Queen, that she had taken the air out of the room.

'May I give you some feedback on what you just said?' Bec asked politely.

'Ah, yes', replied the Queen cautiously, sensing there was no way out.

Bec wrote the word REAL on the whiteboard.

She pointed to the R.'When you gave Dominic feedback what *really* happened was instead of offering reinforcements or giving him something constructive to work on, you just criticised his ability and pointed out something that was wrong.'

'The *effect*', she said, pointing to the E, 'is that Dominic is much less likely to take a risk next time and I doubt that he will easily trust you as a coach in the future'. Bec pointed to the A. 'I need to *ask* you two things. Firstly, can you see how your feedback might have these negative effects?'

The Queen tried to evade the question, but Bec persisted until she reluctantly acknowledged that the feedback she gave was rather personal and not exactly best-practice coaching when you'd been asked to give a reinforcement.

'Now my second question: can I ask that you use the REAL Script in the future so that your feedback is constructive?'

'Of course', replied the Queen. 'But what does the L stand for?'

'*Lift*', replied Bec.'To remind us that good coaches leave people positive and looking forward after giving critical or corrective feedback.'

She turned to the Queen, who was looking a little shell-shocked. 'It's great that you had the courage to give corrective feedback, and I am sure that with some practice and coaching from your colleagues you can refine your technique and become a very effective coach.'

The Queen was now feeling rather pleased with herself, but there was much more to come.

Bec summarised what everyone had seen, repeated the details of what she called the REAL Script, and then asked the Queen to seek Dominic's okay to give him corrective feedback again.

'Dominic,' the Queen began, 'may I offer suggestions on how you can improve?'

'Sure', replied Dominic, bracing himself for another spray.

'What you *really* did was to drop the yoyo rather than giving it a flick, which meant the *effect* was to lose speed, which didn't give you time to form the cradle before the yoyo stopped spinning. Can I *ask* you, were you aware of that and can you focus on giving it a better flick next time?'

Dominic replied that indeed he could make that improvement.

The Queen paused for a moment, considering what to say to lift Dominic's confidence and leave him looking forward. 'I think that you're not far away from getting it right, so with some practice I'm sure you can make it work.'

Applause rose spontaneously from the group as everyone could see how disarmingly effective the REAL Script could be, even in the hands of someone who was naturally critical.

'From dumper to developer', thought Santa, writing furiously in his notebook, while Georgie mused that there was more thinking to be done about the donut and the hole.

reinforce RITE

Bec knew from the survey that preceded the Everyone Coaches workshop that the Sales and Marketing team thought that giving positive reinforcement was easy, but they weren't doing it very well or very often. To tackle this issue she introduced a similar tool to REAL, explaining it by using *RITE* and putting the details on the flip chart.

R is for what the person did that was <u>really</u> positive

I is for the <u>impact</u> of the person's positive action

T is to <u>thank</u> the person for doing this

E is to <u>encourage</u> the person

To reinforce this simple tool she asked the Queen to get Dominic's feedback on her REAL Script.

Dominic obliged. 'You gave me some constructive things to work on (R) and you did it in a way that was really motivating (I), so thanks for the feedback (T) and please feel free to keep on doing that any time you see something that I can do better (E).'

The team broke into small groups, and then used the fun activity of playing with yoyos to get comfortable with using REAL to correct behaviour, and RITE to reinforce behaviour.

Bec had developed this simple Everyone Coaches 'Think Yoyos' activity after years of running boring workshops on feedback and performance reviews. Amazingly, these people will get much more proficient and comfortable in feedback tools and skills by coaching colleagues, friends and family in yoyo techniques than they will ever get from a typical business course.

the prescription

Santa and Georgie were confident that Everyone Coaches was the ideal way to begin equipping people for feedback conversations. They loved the skills of Receive–Reflect–Respond, the simplicity of the two tools REAL and RITE, and the opportunity to do more detailed work on what Bec called REAL Scripts for Tough Conversations.

'It will be perfect for tackling those long-overdue conversations with Ted and HR Harry', thought Santa, and the idea of 'inviting feedback' might just be the breakthrough to cure a whole lot of the ills of the performance review. That was assuming, of course, that they kept the review at all.

As everyone else filed out for lunch, Santa looked at the updated prescription.

The prescription		
For bureaucracy: align	**For ill-equipped people: equip**	**For fear of feedback: partner**
True North	Invite Feedback	Feedback Expectation
	Receive–Reflect–Respond	
	REAL and RITE Scripts	

The prescription looked good but there were still lots of questions running through his head: 'Is that really enough to get past the fear of feedback? Will we have to abolish the performance review to get people to be truly open and honest? How can we create the conversations so that people actually use their coaching skills?'

By the end of the day he would have the answer to some of those questions, and remarkably it would be the Queen who made it happen.

how do you handle critical feedback?

The way we respond to critical feedback, whether valid, invalid or fuzzy, will go a long way to setting the tone for open and honest, or guarded and shallow conversations about behaviour and performance.

Think of a time when you have received some challenging critical feedback, and then use the following questionnaire to reflect on how effectively you handled it.

questionnaire: how did you handle critical feedback?

	Appro-priately	Okay	Inappro-priately
1 Accepted that this was a real issue	☐	☐	☐
2 Reacted quickly	☐	☐	☐
3 Sought to calmly understand the details	☐	☐	☐
4 Showed constructive body language	☐	☐	☐
5 Defended your position	☐	☐	☐
6 Used an excuse to justify or rationalise	☐	☐	☐
7 Sent the message that you are open for feedback	☐	☐	☐
8 Committed to dealing with the issue if valid	☐	☐	☐

how do you handle critical feedback? *(cont'd)*

Here are six strategies to improve the way you handle critical feedback:

→ *Seek feedback early and often.* The longer the gaps in communication the more difficult it can be to handle criticism, so seek feedback early and often.

→ *Invite feedback.* The concept of inviting or 'pulling' feedback takes away the onus on the giver of feedback, who like most people is probably holding back on being open and honest. It also gives you more sense of control over what you are being told.

→ *Understand the detail.* Without showing defensiveness try to understand exactly what people are telling you because the more specific the feedback and the better you understand the critique, the easier it is to make the improvement.

→ *Consider the validity.* Not all sources of feedback are equal, so there is no point in getting upset over invalid feedback. It is one of the reasons many athletes don't read the newspaper — they don't want their self-esteem affected by people who have other agendas or no real insight.

→ *Take your medicine.* Few things magnify an error or a poor performance more than a person who conceals, denies or plays down the issue. If you've performed poorly, then simply accept the feedback, take your medicine and move on.

→ *Don't exaggerate.* At times of pressure or stress we all have a tendency to exaggerate issues. Doing so can cause overly emotional reactions, feelings of hopelessness and an inability to choose the right response. Friends, colleagues and time can all help us to gain a better perspective.

The foundation is now set to invite the truth.

chapter 11

the elephant in the room

Everyone came back from lunch energised from the morning's activity but acutely aware that this was the session where the rubber really hit the road. Bec had taken Santa and Georgie aside during the break to chat about their insights on the performance review and to explain the afternoon activity that she called Feedback Circles.

They both were eager to see the 'real' feedback conversations, but Bec had some words of caution before they began. 'The activity this afternoon is just one part of the Feedback Circles process and this group will be quite a bit further advanced than where you'll start with lots of other companies', she explained.

'Why is that?' asked Georgie.

'They've been using a framework called think one team for about two years, and one of the keys to that is regular debriefing between teams and team leaders. They're accustomed to holding debriefing sessions where people give and receive feedback.'

'How does debriefing work?' asked Santa

'Well, think one team is basically teamwork across boundaries, so that's achieved through forming partnerships. That starts by aligning expectations between people and departments. We keep them aligned by debriefing using specially designed templates based on four core questions: What was supposed to happen? What actually happened? What were the differences? How can we learn and improve? Let's talk more about it later', suggested Bec as the last of the team members arrived back in the room.

The afternoon was nothing short of a revelation for Santa, as people worked in groups of about eight and used their debriefing skills and the newly acquired coaching skills to have some of the most open and tough performance conversations he had ever seen. One particular mid-afternoon exchange in the 'feedback circles' was a highlight.

feedback circles

Jimmy Chew knew that as Head of Sales and Marketing he set the tone for the depth of honesty he could expect from his team. Choosing one of the options from what Bec called the Feedback Circles menu, Jimmy posed a question to the group of colleagues with whom he was seated and then left the room for ten minutes while they considered their thoughts. (The word 'colleagues' was part of the language used throughout the workshop to minimise the effects of differences in status).

The question Jimmy had posed and that they had accepted as specific and relevant was: 'Am I doing enough to address the poorer performers in this team?'

It was a loaded question because for the team to be truly honest they had to identify exactly what Jimmy was not doing, and that meant potentially identifying the colleagues whom Jimmy wasn't addressing. Ten minutes wasn't long but it helped to get people over the tendency to procrastinate.

Jimmy returned and began by providing the self-assessment that he had jotted down outside. 'My feeling is that I am ninety per cent of the way there,' he said, 'but I want to know what that other ten per cent is and if I need to do something about it'.

With a room full of people trained to coach there was no way that Jimmy could just leave his comment at that point.

'What do you think that ten per cent is?' asked Tracey.

Jimmy paused to reflect and to choose his words carefully. 'Values', he said pausing again. 'I think there are some people in this team who are not living the values and I should be having open and honest conversations with them.'

There was silence as people thought about what he had said.

'Why aren't you having the conversations?' asked Dominic.

'Good question,' replied Jimmy, 'but before I answer it, I need your feedback on whether I'm valid in my self-assessment'.

Following the rules, the team turned over the flip chart sheet that summarised their views.

Tracey explained each point. 'If we use the REAL Script from this morning, then one thing that is *really* happening, Jimmy, is that you haven't been clear enough with each of us about the standards of teamwork that you expect. The *effect* is that people have different views about what is or isn't acceptable. We each agreed that we need to *ask* you if you are aware of this, and we want it looked at because it's causing some unnecessary friction between people. We all agreed that we have huge respect for your leadership and we think this will make things even better.'

Santa watched carefully to see the reaction and it wasn't entirely what he expected.

'Thank you', replied Jimmy with humility. 'Can I ask a couple of questions?'

'Of course', replied Tracey.

'In which specific areas of teamwork are there different expectations?'

'Mostly around sharing information and being prepared to put aside personal agendas for the bigger picture', replied one of the product managers.

'Haven't I made that clear?'

The Queen, whose real name was Denise, had been shuffling uncomfortably but saw an opening and took it.

'I thought you had been crystal clear', she commented to raised eyebrows in the group.

'So why didn't you say that before?' asked Dominic tersely.

'Because no-one asked me', Denise replied sarcastically.

Jimmy could see things were beginning to unravel, but knew it usually meant that a breakthrough was close. 'Denise, I agree with part of what you are saying and I feel that I have been clear about standards, but I wonder whether what I haven't been clear about is the responsibility on everyone to call behaviours that don't meet those standards. What do you think, Hamish?' Jimmy asked to the surprise of the graduate who reported to Denise.

'Yeah, I think what has happened here is exactly the behaviour that we are sick and tired of. Denise wasn't open with the team, and then said something different to your face. That happens quite often and not just with Denise, so I guess you've got to take some responsibility for that.'

Santa sat back, not quite believing that the youngest and least-experienced person in the room had given the most senior person in the room and his boss a serve of honesty that had both of them reeling.

Denise started to speak but Jimmy interrupted her.

'Thank you, Hamish. Denise and I are going to step outside for a few minutes. I appreciate your feedback, but I think this needs some time for the reflect and respond part of Bec's model.'

The Queen was obviously fuming. It was a smart call on Jimmy's part.

taking the elephant outside the room

As soon as they were in the corridor Denise began attacking Hamish and promising to deliver his head on a platter. Jimmy let her go on before stopping her in her tracks with one sentence.

'Denise, the only person in this company who is likely to get an 'A' on their performance review is Hamish because he has done exactly what we have asked him to do — give feedback, openly and honestly.'

'But what about the way he criticised me in front of everyone?'

'Okay, maybe Hamish could be a little more polished in his delivery, but I'm betting that he's as open to that feedback as he is to giving it. More important is how you and I are going to go back into that room and show the others that we are serious about making open and honest conversations the number one priority in this business.'

'You're kidding', said an incredulous Denise.

'No, I'm not', replied Jimmy, who for the first time really understood why the decision to make open and honest feedback the only performance criteria was brilliant.

It simply cut away all the other fluff and made people focus on what was real. It certainly had some risks, but he genuinely could see the almost limitless potential of a team that had eliminated the fear of feedback.

'I'm going back in there to admit that you have been the elephant in the room that I have not been dealing with.'

Denise was speechless.

'Now, we can go back in together and admit that together, or you can try it your way.'

'What am I supposed to admit?' asked Denise, still hoping she could evade the scrutiny that her blunt manner and power suit had kept at bay for most of her career.

'That you have not been honest with your colleagues and I have let you get away with it.'

Denise sat. Jimmy waited. 'I can't!' she finally exclaimed.

'Why not?' asked Jimmy gently.

'Because they'll think I'm a fraud.'

'Perhaps they'll think exactly the opposite. Denise, if you go back into that room and make up some excuse, then they will think you're a fraud, but if you are totally honest they'll cut you some slack.'

A few more moments passed.

'Let's do it', encouraged Jimmy, not sure what Denise would say but committed to being open and honest himself.

They re-entered a quiet room and rejoined their group.

This time Jimmy started to speak but Denise stopped him.

'I want to apologise', she began, showing more humanity than anyone had ever seen from her. 'I have not been honest with you. I am the elephant in the room. I am the person who doesn't fit with the way this team wants to play the game. It's time for me to leave.'

She stood.

'Wait', said Dominic.'That's the most courageous thing I've seen for a long time. It's not time for you to leave, Denise, it's time for you to really join the team.'

She put her head in her hands.

'Wow', thought Santa.'Imagine the possibilities if everyone could have open and honest conversations such as these, every day.'

the prescription

Adding Feedback Circles to the prescription made Santa much more confident that they had not only the skills to equip people, but also at least one way to bring people together to tackle those difficult conversations.

Santa and Georgie would have loved to spend more time with the team at O'Donnell's Jelly Bean Company, particularly discussing the different levels of Feedback Circles, but Brad's last email had said that Ralph was putting pressure on for immediate changes. Time was running out. They had to get back to Lapland and put the cure in place before Ralph got his way and did some major surgery on the business. Hopefully they could fill in the remaining spaces before it was too late.

The prescription		
For bureaucracy: align	For ill-equipped people: equip	For fear of feedback: partner
True North	Invite Feedback	Feedback Expectation
	Receive-Reflect-Respond	Feedback Circles
	REAL and RITE Scripts	

handling the elephants in your office

Complete the following questionnaire to discover whether you are likely to have trained a few elephants to sit around the office!

questionnaire: my attitudes and behaviours to critical feedback

	Never	Rarely	Some-times	Often	Always
1 I avoid opportunities to give my boss critical feedback.	☐	☐	☐	☐	☐
2 Colleagues are too busy to want my feedback.	☐	☐	☐	☐	☐
3 I let things sort themselves out before giving challenging feedback to direct reports.	☐	☐	☐	☐	☐
4 I don't give feedback if people are likely to react emotionally.	☐	☐	☐	☐	☐

	Never	Rarely	Some-times	Often	Always
5 My staff and colleagues know when I'm not happy so giving specific feedback isn't needed.	☐	☐	☐	☐	☐
6 Performance reviews are the best time to tackle major behavioural issues.	☐	☐	☐	☐	☐
7 Giving feedback damages relationships.	☐	☐	☐	☐	☐

If you look carefully at your responses, the 'often' and 'always' ratings will tell you whether there are any possible elephants among your boss, colleagues or direct reports.

Don't shoot the elephants!

speed dating

Sometimes ideas come from the strangest places, although not even Georgie could have expected one of their biggest breakthrough ideas to come from one of her craziest expeditions.

After leaving O'Donnell's Jelly Bean Company with a promise to return with the 'cure', the travellers had a final stopover in London before flying on to Lapland.

And it would have been the quiet two days that Santa expected if Georgie was not so unlucky in love. Work always seemed to take first place in her priorities. She needed to find a way to meet the right partner.

As fate would have it Georgie strolled into an internet café and while surfing the net came across an advertisement for speed dating for people seeking partners in London. 'What a perfect way to meet people in a short space of time', she thought, while hastily typing in contact details to make a booking for that evening. It was the final line that caught her attention. It read: 'If you feel a little self-conscious, why not bring a friend?'

Her mischievous mind went into overdrive. 'He'll kill me', she giggled as she entered the jolly man from Lapland into the speed dating function.

Later that day on the pretence of going out to dinner, Georgie had seated her blissfully unaware travelling companion comfortably in the back of a London cab. They were booked into a speed dating party for twenty people, but it would only happen if the great man agreed, and Georgie knew that she had to tell him at least some time in advance — although five minutes was perhaps a little short notice.

'Er, GM,' she began, 'there's something about this restaurant that I need to explain'.

Georgie tried to play on Santa's good nature, but by the time they reached the venue, it was clear that he still didn't really understand his role in the evening.

'So, while you do this speed dating thing what am I supposed to do?' he asked, more concerned about food than whatever Georgie was going on about.

'Well, that's the thing GM', she said. 'You're doing it too.'

'Doing what?' he asked abruptly.

'Speed dating. You know, having five-minute conversations with ten women.'

'What?!' he exploded with a mix of rage and panic.

'Oh come on', she pleaded. 'It'll be fun, and you always like meeting new people.'

'No', he replied with less conviction.

But Georgie's persuasive powers and the happy coincidence that they met the equally persuasive and also charming host, Lesley, on the steps of the restaurant, led Santa to be seated opposite a forty-something divorcee from Bournemouth with a penchant for travelling to tropical islands.

Each person was given a card on which potential partners' names were mentioned together with a speed rating system that allowed them to record initial impressions in four categories.

Santa found some of the conversations excruciating, but he did meet three ladies with whom he found things in common, and under sufferance he admitted later to Georgie that he quite enjoyed the experience.

Georgie had to be dragged away from a conversation with Todd, a fireman from Paddington. Remarkably all ten ladies had Todd top of their list, but his completed rating card confirmed that there was no-one he would like to see again.

Georgie was locked in her room, her hopes dashed again.

It was late the next afternoon before she emerged, and she and Santa agreed that a drink at the bar might be in order.

The conversation quickly jumped to the previous evening's experience and they started to laugh. It was exactly what Georgie needed to cheer her up.

'You know those speed dating cards', said Santa.

'Yep', replied Georgie, sipping on a vodka with lemon.

'Well, we know that a key to curing the performance review is to get people to pull feedback regularly.'

Georgie nodded, not sure where this was going.

'What if everyone had a card that they used to invite feedback from their boss once every two months?'

'What would be on the card?' she asked.

'I'm not settled on this,' he replied, 'but I've always said that there are four things I expect from everyone in my company'.

'Let me guess', said Georgie, who knew the Santa creed extremely well. 'Do your job, serve your customer, support your team, be engaged.'

'Exactly. So we could replace the review with a sort of speed rating or maybe speed review, where staff pull feedback from the managers.'

'That's a brilliant idea!' she replied excitedly. 'And at the same time, the managers could invite feedback on the two things that they must do in order to be good coaches.'

'And they are?'

'Give direction and provide support.'

'What if we put all that on a card like the one Lesley gave us?' Santa suggested. 'That way we'd have the perfect platform for open performance conversations.'

the prescription

Santa and Georgie looked at each other. GET a Feedback Expectation. Invite Feedback. Speed Review. REAL Scripts for Tough Conversations. RITE Scripts. Feedback Circles.

There were still a couple of things missing, and after a few drinks this wasn't the time to be designing the Speed Review card, but when they got back to Lapland it would be first thing on the agenda. It really was time to go home and pull the cure together.

The prescription		
For bureaucracy: align	**For ill-equipped people: equip**	**For fear of feedback: partner**
True North	Invite Feedback	Feedback Expectation
	Receive–Reflect–Respond	Feedback Circles
	REAL and RITE Scripts	Speed Review

part IV

the cure

chapter 13

plan, do, check, adapt

L ike most engineer-trained leaders Ralph Hampton Jr preferred and had a routine. Every Friday morning at 7.30 sharp he met with his Chief Financial Officer to review the performance of his companies. A typical meeting took two hours—enough time for the dynamic young businessman to pore over the graphs and dashboards that showed the health of his operating companies. This was followed by a ferocious game of racquet ball before a light lunch.

On the last Friday of the month the Xmas Franchise Systems executive team joined Ralph to review the monthly performance. The New York–based members made the early morning trip into Manhattan, while the chief executives of the operating companies dialled in on video conference. It was usually a short, sharp review of key metrics and any major exceptions. Ralph led the discussions and expected his team to be on top of the numbers for their businesses. Those who weren't did not enjoy the monthly review.

On the last Friday of each quarter the whole team assembled in New York for a major review at which any discrepancies from the quarterly plan were dissected and analysed, and an action plan agreed on. In the morning there was a group activity, and then in the afternoon Ralph met each chief executive individually.

Every six months the team stayed for the Saturday to discuss future opportunities, and once a year on the last Friday in August the team met at an upmarket business resort for a four-day strategic and operational planning retreat, at which new strategies and tactics were debated and the business plan defined and confirmed.

'PDCA', expounded Ralph to his high-powered team every week, month, quarter, biannually and annually. 'We base our planning on the simple, elegant and powerful method given to the world by W Edwards Deming, the father of quality control.'

On a wall in Ralph's office hung a Van Gogh and a rather plain poster that showed the all-important cycle that Deming had created to apply the scientific method of testing a hypothesis to the world of business manufacturing. Ralph valued the plain poster more than the Van Gogh. From the day he applied PDCA to Donut Delicacies he knew that he could have as many Van Goghs as he wanted, provided he remained loyal to PDCA.

Ralph didn't follow Deming's original cycle, which read Plan–Do–Study–Act. Ralph was not interested in studying or acting. He wanted his managers to plan, do, check and adapt—fast.

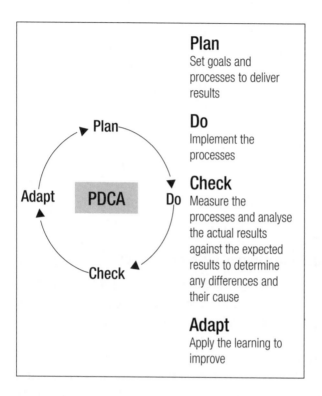

Plan
Set goals and processes to deliver results

Do
Implement the processes

Check
Measure the processes and analyse the actual results against the expected results to determine any differences and their cause

Adapt
Apply the learning to improve

not good enough

Since moving from Orlando to NewYork Ralph had devoted every day of his life to two words:'own Christmas'.

The cash flow from Donut Delicacies when combined with his financiers, willing contributions enabled him to buy the string of businesses that gave him control of what he called the'total Christmas experience'. But as he pored over the numbers this particular Friday morning Ralph shook his head. Santa Enterprises was haemorrhaging money despite its massive product licensing portfolio, his beloved Donut Delicacies had dropped to number two in market share and was heading south, and Send Cards! would struggle to break even this quarter.

This was not just the lingering effects of the recession. It couldn't be. He'd promised his financiers a recession-proof business. They owned the franchise that gave Santa Claus to the world. They owned Christmas. It was the perfect business model. But it was not making money.

The numbers might have been heading south, but on Saturday morning Ralph Hampton Jr was heading north to meet with Brad Smyth, Chief Executive of Santa Enterprises. It was time for a proper performance review with Mr Smyth. And, Ralph thought with some anticipation, with Mr Claus.

---

is PDCA a part of the prescription?

Ralph isn't thinking about using his beloved PDCA to cure the ills of the performance review; however, the XFS business planning cycle is actually built on the four stages — plan, do, check, adapt.

While simply reciting PDCA won't change anything, XFS has this feedback loop hard-wired into its business performance system. This means there is a great opportunity to include a 'people performance PDCA', rather than having a 'performance management system' and 'performance review', which are separate and run by the HR department to a different time cycle. The following points illustrate how PDCA fits into the people performance cycle.

→ **Plan** — Staff member and manager agree on personal goals, which are aligned to the True North for the team and overall business.

→ **Do** — Day-to-day performance and coaching are aligned to the plans.

→ **Check** — Regular performance conversations, including the speed review and the longer-term review of goals and development plans, enable learning to occur.

→ **Adapt**—What is learned is applied to improve performance in the next PDCA cycle.

Using a 'people PDCA' provides the opportunity to pull the performance conversations into the same time cycles that happen in the business. This has many potential benefits, including better goal alignment and the likelihood that feedback will happen when and where it is needed, rather than through a 'too late' performance review.

The following questionnaire will help you to reflect on whether the PDCA cycle is a natural part of the way your business operates.

---

questionnaire: is PDCA happening in your business?

	Never	Rarely	Some-times	Often	Always
1 We set clear plans for each performance cycle.	☐	☐	☐	☐	☐
2 We align our day-to-day actions to those plans.	☐	☐	☐	☐	☐
3 We regularly and thoroughly debrief performance.	☐	☐	☐	☐	☐
4 We use the learning from the debriefing to improve.	☐	☐	☐	☐	☐

is PDCA a part of the prescription? *(cont'd)*

If you ticked 'Often' or 'Always' for each item, you have an effective PDCA feedback loop, which means you are well placed to align the planning and review cycles for both people performance and business performance. If you ticked 'Sometimes', 'Rarely' or 'Never' for any item, you will need to strengthen the business planning and review cycle before trying to align the 'people cycle'.

Can PDCA be part of curing the ills of your performance review?

no fear

As soon as they saw Brad in the airport arrival hall on Friday evening Santa and Georgie sensed immediately that something was wrong. Their final hours in London and on the plane had been spent excitedly finalising their plan to cure the performance review at Santa Enterprises, but the look on Brad's face quickly changed their mood.

After some pressing he shared his worries with them in the car ride back to the village. He sounded defeated. 'The numbers from the past few weeks are terrible. XFS is demanding immediate action. The whole group took a pounding in the last quarter. They aren't interested in anything but a quick fix.'

Santa knew what that meant but Georgie wanted the details. 'What are you saying?' she asked.

Brad gulped. 'We have to retrench about twenty per cent of the workforce, and that doesn't include all the contractors that usually do the basic maintenance in the quieter months.'

'Twenty per cent!?' exclaimed Santa, who hadn't been expecting anything like that.

'Are there any alternatives?' asked Georgie.

'Well, it gets worse.'

'How?'

'Ralph will be here tomorrow afternoon and he's got Phil Sprinkler and me locked away in a room to do one of his PDCA activities on our businesses and ...', he hesitated.

'And?' prompted Georgie.

'And he's demanding to do a performance review on you, Santa.'

'What does that mean, GM?' asked Georgie with alarm.

'It means we've got less than twenty-four hours to put our prescription together in a format that will convince Mr Hampton that this business has a future without having to slash and burn.'

'I'm pretty sure that Ralph doesn't want to discuss how to cure the performance review, Santa. He wants to do one on you, and I think it's going to be pretty pointed if I know Ralph.'

'Brad,' said Santa in a more confident and business-like tone than anyone had ever heard before, 'if Mr Hampton is coming here for an open and honest conversation, then he will not be disappointed'.

Brad looked at him curiously. Something had fundamentally changed and it wasn't just the remnants of the Bondi Beach suntan. There was a calm confidence. He hadn't realised it before, but Santa had always seemed anxious and fearful of something. And now that fear had gone.

from review to preview

It was Saturday morning. Ralph Hampton Jr was already on his way to Lapland in seat 1A of a British Airways 747, when the great man and Georgie joined Brad and Phil Sprinker at head office.

'Before we go into detail, can I get straight to the point?' asked Phil with more than a hint of urgency.

'Of course', replied Brad. 'What do you need?'

'Bottom line,' said Phil bluntly, looking at Santa and Georgie, 'have you found anything that's going to make a quick and significant difference to our business performance? Because I'd rather use the next four hours to work on the numbers if this is going to be a long-term HR solution'.

'I hear what you're saying, but we have to deal with this sometime', said Brad in a more conciliatory tone.

'Just a minute', interrupted Santa.

'I appreciate your support and that you are under a lot of pressure, but we have found what you asked for and yes, Phil, we have found more.'

'Have we?' thought Georgie, not quite sure where Santa was going with this.

'You should spend the morning on the things that you think are most important, though.'

'Sorry, Santa. I didn't mean to upset you', explained Phil, realising he'd gone too far.

'Phil, I'm not the least bit upset', replied Santa, yet again surprising Brad with his calm confidence.

'What Georgie and I would prefer is that you and Brad do what you need to do to prepare for your meeting with Mr Hampton. All I ask is one thing.'

'Sure, what's that?' asked Brad.

'Please tell Mr Hampton that Georgie and I want to do his performance review between 2.00 and 3.30 this afternoon.'

There was not a sound or movement in the room for thirty seconds. No-one, not even Georgie, had a clue what to say or what Santa was thinking.

Ralph Hampton Jr might be relatively young, but he ate business managers like Santa Claus for breakfast. Did Santa think he was indispensable? Well, he probably was, but then there were at last count almost one million franchised Santas in the shopping malls of the world, so no doubt Ralph could find one that suited his needs.

'Santa, maybe the jet lag ...'

The great man stopped Brad mid sentence. 'Give me a moment.' He stood without saying anything further and left the room.

'Is he ill?' asked Phil, wondering if he'd picked up something on his travels.

'No', said Georgie. 'He was as bright and bubbly as I have seen him for years when we headed over to the glass castle this morning.'

'Hampton's going kill him', said Brad, just as Santa re-entered the room.

'This afternoon at 2.00. I just confirmed it with his personal assistant.'

'What exactly did you confirm with her?' asked Brad, nonplussed.

Santa could see that the Chief Executive doubted his intentions, so he repeated it again. 'Georgie and I will be doing Mr Hampton's performance review at 2.00 this afternoon.'

Georgie's eyes widened. The old guy obviously had delayed heat stroke from Bondi Beach.

'That's it? No further explanation?' Brad asked with concern for Santa's welfare.

'Only that you and Phil are also expected to attend.'

'I think this is enough', said Phil, who was starting to loose his cool with the great man.

But Santa hadn't finished yet.

'Phil, do you trust me?'

It was quite a question to be asked by Santa Claus.

'Of course', replied Phil as a reflex.

'No,' insisted Santa, 'do you really trust me to do the right thing by all of us this afternoon with Mr Hampton?'

Phil paused and thought for a while.

'No, I don't, because I think you're such a nice guy that you don't know what you're getting yourself into with Ralph Hampton when he's looking for blood.'

'Thank you', replied Santa. 'Thank you for telling me the truth. I appreciate your feedback but I will still be going into that meeting and I'd like you to come because anyone who can tell Santa Claus to his face that he doesn't trust him is a person to be trusted.'

Georgie was impressed. 'Wow', she thought. 'This new Santa rocks!'

Phil could do nothing but agree. Brad half smiled. Could this be the same person he spoke to just a few weeks ago? That person shrank from the truth. This person invited it, accepted it and if he was any judge, was going to a meeting this afternoon to speak it.

ralph's review

'Santa.'

'Mr Hampton.'

'Have you met Georgie?' asked Brad, introducing the blonde dynamo.

'No, we haven't met, but I have heard about you from Bud Eldon.'

'Damn', thought Georgie. 'I'm toast.'

Pleasantries aside, Santa asked Mr Hampton Jr to take a few minutes to explain the reason for his visit, and then to participate in his performance review.

For all his reputation as a tough businessman Ralph didn't get rich and stay rich without a strong mix of good judgement, courage and chutzpah. He admired Santa for having the courage to put the performance review on the table. He was here for the weekend, so he'd play along to see if there was value to be had.

It took just twenty minutes for Ralph to paint a picture of an XFS business that was not as recession-proof as his salivating financiers expected. Staff turnover, a drop in quality and changes in competitors' behaviour due to the economic downturn had all eaten into profits. Add to that the continuing high cost of capital.

Ralph concluded, 'We have three months to meet the numbers that my financiers are expecting or drastic action will have to be taken'.

The others didn't ask what 'drastic action' meant, but historically it meant removing the power of the chief executives of the operating companies, putting in someone with all the attributes of a serial killer and letting them carry out the bodies.

'Mr Hampton,' began Santa in an earnest tone, 'you may be aware that Brad asked Georgie and me to find a cure for the ills of the performance review'.

Ralph gave an expressionless nod.

'We found that the performance review sits at the centre of four fundamental business problems that are afflicting at least three of your businesses — staff productivity, customer satisfaction, teamwork on key initiatives and staff turnover.' Santa handed him a sheet of paper with the four items on it.

Ralph couldn't let the comment pass without challenge. 'How can the review be at the centre of the problems? That doesn't make sense. Reviews don't cause problems. Reviews fix problems.'

'I said it was at the centre', replied Santa. 'I didn't say it was the cause.'

The Managing Director wasn't a man who appreciated having his time wasted.

'So, get to the point.'

'Do you agree that you have those four problems?'

'Of course, that's what I just told you.'

'And do you know the cause?' asked Santa.

'If I knew the cause,' retorted Ralph, starting to lose his cool, 'I wouldn't be sitting here in this freezing place listening to Santa Claus'.

Georgie almost laughed out loud at how ridiculous that sounded. It wouldn't have been good timing on her part, particularly given what Santa was about to say.

'The cause is you, Mr Hampton.'

Ralph's eyes widened.

'And it's me, and Mr Smyth and Mr Sprinkler.'

Ralph's blood pressure dropped slightly, but no-one in the room was breathing, so Santa needed to explain — fast.

'You've seen the movie *A Few Good Men*?'

It was Ralph's favourite movie. 'Yes.'

'You know that scene where Jack Nicholson tells Tom Cruise that he can't handle the truth?'

'Yes, so?'

'Well, we have created an organisation of people who can't handle the truth.'

'Go on', said Ralph.

'We have put in what HR calls a "performance management system", which is supposed to tell us the truth about how the business and its people are performing. But that assumes one thing.'

'Which is?'

'That people can handle the truth. But they can't. I have done it all my life', explained Santa with breathtaking candour. 'I have always avoided telling the truth in case it upsets someone. I have always avoided seeking the truth about me in case someone actually told me the truth.'

Everyone sat stunned.

'If you want to fix this company, Mr Hampton, we have the cure but *you* have to take it.'

'What is it?'

Santa handed out copies of the prescription. It had been completed by adding PDCA cycles and some Principles of Align, which they would shortly share with their colleagues.

The prescription		
For bureaucracy: align	**For ill-equipped people: equip**	**For fear of feedback: partner**
True North	Invite Feedback	Feedback Expectation
PDCA Cycles	Receive-Reflect-Respond	Feedback Circles
Principles of Align	REAL and RITE Scripts	Speed Review

'Please let Georgie and me explain, and then give us three months to implement the prescription across Santa Enterprises and Donut Delicacies. If you don't see a substantial and continuing improvement in performance after that time, then you will have my resignation.'

Ralph knew a good deal when he saw it, but the businessman was still sceptical.

'What's going to change in three months?'

'Georgie and I will create a program called *cure the review*. It won't require a single dollar spent on systems because what we do will bolt onto HR Harry's masterpiece. What we'll need is a website and two skilled facilitators to bring this to life.'

'That's all good and well,' acknowledged the tenth wealthiest man in the United States, 'but you're still not telling me what's going to change'.

'Performance', replied Georgie, joining in. 'Your companies are awash with things just waiting to be fixed. Give us the chance and your own people will cut costs, boost service and give you the extra cash that's needed to get through these tough times. We just need to stop avoiding having the tough conversation and start dealing with the truth.'

Ralph paused. Georgie didn't. She was on a roll.

'Take Sleigh Maintenance, for example', she implored. 'Let's get Ted in here for a *real* conversation about the difference between bullying and partnering. Let's give him and everyone else a True North so they don't drift off on their own agenda. Let's create the feedback expectation so that people expect continual improvement every day. Let's stop waiting for feedback and instead invite feedback every day.'

'And give me the chance to have a real conversation with Bud Eldon', added Phil, acutely aware that he personally needed to implement the cure and stop avoiding the tough conversations.

'Imagine the possibilities of feedback circles across the whole business', said Brad. 'No more waiting for the review to get or give feedback, no more people just talking about having the tough conversation. Actually having it because people want the truth and they know how to handle it.'

'Done', agreed Ralph, who had heard enough. 'What do you need?' he asked Santa.

'We need your help this weekend. And', he addressed Phil and Brad, 'we need all of you to mandate one thing to make this work'.

'What's the one thing you want mandated?' asked Brad, curious at this request.

'Georgie and I will explain in more detail, but from everything we've done we believe that the one thing that has to happen is monthly one-on-one feedback conversations between managers and staff. We believe these should be mandatory and not left to managers or staff to say they are too busy or travelling or using some other excuse.'

'How long does that meeting need to be?' asked Ralph.

'Maximum thirty minutes', replied Georgie.

'Is that long enough?'

'Yes', said Santa, thinking of speed dating and their brilliant little speed review cards.

'Done', announced Ralph again.

the first three pieces

Ralph looked at the prescription and the three key words —align, equip, partner. It made sense: *align* True North with his beloved PDCA cycles and a set of principles; *equip* people to be coaches who are skilled and comfortable to invite, offer and accept feedback; create *partner*ships between managers and direct reports, and between colleagues built on a feedback expectation and sustained by speed reviews and feedback circles.

'We need your help this weekend to do the align part, and then we can implement from there', advised Santa.

'Let's get on with it then', encouraged the Managing Director.

And so, the small and highly capable team set to work, each secretly hoping that they could replace the bureaucracy of the ineffective and tired performance review with a simple and elegant alternative.

true north at last

For True North the team created a framework in the form of templates that would be placed on the website for everyone to use and to cascade a consistent big picture throughout the XFS companies.

Four questions provided the framework for True North:

- Why are we here?

- What must we achieve?

- How will we achieve those things?

- What values and principles will guide us?

Having a clear True North meant that every department and team could use the same simple and consistent language and process in their business planning. True North would align the business and connect everyone to a clear set of expectations. That would then enable every manager and every staff member to implement the GET, a Feedback Expectation tool that Santa and Georgie had created after their lesson with Mr Peng in Singapore.

Having a feedback expectation would reduce the fear of feedback and, when combined with the coaching skills and mandatory one-on-one conversations, would mean that instead of avoidance they could push a new mantra: 'Feedback—do it early and do it often'.

speed reviews

It was so obvious when you thought about it that Ralph used PDCA cycles (weekly, monthly, quarterly, six monthly and annual) to review the business performance and plan ahead, so why not use the same cycles for staff perform-ance reviews? The weekly, monthly and quarterly meetings were mainly 'Do–Check' activities and as the time frame increased the conversations changed to 'Plan–Adapt'. 'From review to preview', as Ralph liked to describe it.

'So we need a way to do the real performance review every one or two months, and then we can use the six- and twelve-month cycles to preview or plan future development and performance', said Ralph.

'That's why we recommend mandating a mini-review monthly between leaders and their direct reports', explained Georgie.

Phil nodded but observed, 'The managers will definitely complain that they're too busy'.

'Yes, they will', confirmed Georgie. 'However, there are two issues with that. Firstly, making the regular one-on-one mandatory, and secondly, having a simple tool to empower people to do it quickly and effectively.'

She saw the expression on Santa's face, which read clearly, 'Don't you even think about mentioning speed dating', and kept moving.

'We have developed a simple tool called Speed Review that managers and staff can use to have twenty-minute two-way conversations that will cover the four big performance issues — productivity, service, teamwork and engagement.'

'And the two critical leadership issues — direction and support', added Santa, handing them an example of the card, on which was written 'Speed Review' — although for some reason Georgie had called it speed dating more than once, and that seemed to turn the jolly man bright red for no apparent reason.

'So explain this one to me again. And how did you think this up?' asked Phil of Georgie and Santa, who looked at each other like two rabbits in the car headlights.

Santa took the lead. 'Ah, well, it was just something we thought up because the performance review systems are so bureaucratic and we felt that something was needed that could be used to have quick, two-way conversations without getting too bogged down with rating scales.'

Phil nodded. 'I think it's brilliant, but I'm curious why Georgie keeps calling it speed dating.'

'Oh,' said Georgie, quick to cover up, 'I sometimes get my Ds and Rs mixed up'.

Santa grimaced. Brad knew something was up but obviously the co-conspirators weren't going to give it up easily.

Finally the attention shifted to the Speed Review card. It was indeed functional simplicity. Divided into four sections on the left and two on the right it was about the size of a aeroplane boarding pass.

Speed review at / /		
Partners _____	_____	
Do your **JOB**	Support your **TEAM**	Give **DIRECTION**
Serve your **CUSTOMER**	Be **ENGAGED**	Provide **SUPPORT**

The idea was stunningly simple. Put the responsibility on both staff and managers to meet for a partnering meeting once every month for twenty to thirty minutes to complete what Phil jokingly called the 'dance card'. Make the completed cards a KPI for all managers.

Arrows would be drawn in each box to identify the direction of performance in the past month: four elements for the staff member and two (direction and support) for the manager.

Georgie and Santa would provide a set of guidelines that would be introduced in the training sessions so that the monthly reviews fostered the open and honest conversations that had been missing in the past. Other versions had also been designed with specific behaviours to align to HR Harry's system without adding to costs.

'I love it', mused Phil. 'It's perfect for getting around the excuses about not having time to do a review, and it also gives people something tangible to use to direct the conversation.

'I agree', said Brad. 'You can do it face-to-face or even over Skype if needed, so it's a winner. Let's take a break.'

'Great, I look forward to hearing how that works, but if you have any trouble getting managers to do the monthly one-on-ones, then let me know', said Ralph in his best 'I mean this' tone.

principles

When the group reconvened the first to speak was Brad.

'What's going to happen at the six- and twelve-monthly reviews, if that's what we still call them?' he asked.

'Georgie and I debated for a long time whether we should abolish the review altogether', replied Santa. 'We realised pretty quickly that in most companies the review hasn't got a chance because before you even start people are at cross-purposes about what the review is supposed to do.'

'Exactly', jumped in Georgie. 'Most managers think the review is to improve performance while their staff think it's about their career development and salary.'

'And half the people think it's about feedback while the other half think it shouldn't be about feedback at all!' added Santa.

'No wonder it doesn't work', said Phil, as everyone nodded in agreement.

'So we decided to abolish the review.'

'Really?' said Ralph with genuine surprise.

'Well, yes and no', replied Santa. 'The six-month or twelve-month review as people currently know it should go because it just doesn't make sense. It's trying to be a review, a feedback meeting, a career-planning session and so on, all at the same time. That just can't work.

'Our solution is two of the plan–do–check–adapt cycles with a set of principles that will make it a proper people performance and development cycle. In other words, it tackles both the review and preview issues.'

Ralph liked what he was hearing but needed more detail, so Santa explained.

'Cycle one is monthly and focuses on job performance and short-horizon development issues. That's the mandatory one-on-one plus the regular on-the-job performance conversations.

'Cycle two is six monthly, or could be twelve monthly, and focuses on planning for job and career development. That's more aligned to the sort of forward planning that the business does in that cycle. Harry already has the career and job-planning forms needed for that, and the speed reviews will mean that it can be a look forward, rather than look back conversation.'

They looked at the whiteboard where Santa had drawn a simple table.

PDCA cycle	Main tool	Purpose
Monthly	Speed review	To review performance against plan and to make necessary changes.
Six monthly	Performance and development plan	To collate the speed reviews, scan the environment and plan for the next six to twelve months for job and career development.

'What are you going to call it?' Phil asked Georgie.

'We don't think the name is that important', she replied. 'Although the monthly speed review is technically the new performance review, we'd rather lose the words "performance review" and "performance management" because they are pretty negative for staff.'

Phil agreed. 'Why not just call the whole process "Align"?'

They all thought that was a great idea. Keep it simple and lose the negative terms from the past.

'Okay, then these are the Principles of Align', said Santa, handing out another sheet.

'Is that enough?' asked Phil, looking at the single sheet.

Brad understood that the concerns Phil was expressing were on behalf of managers who were accustomed to performance reviews coming with lots of rules. 'One of the problems with the current review is that it is too bureaucratic, so provided we remember that Align is fundamentally about regular performance conversations then the framework and tools will work.'

The purpose of Align is to optimise people performance and development by implementing the prescription

To align	• Align to be owned by the business units — HR sponsors the system and training.
	• Align to be built on two PDCA cycles — man-datory monthly review (maximum thirty minutes) and six-monthly preview (all managers have both as a KPI).
	• Align to begin with each team aligning to True North on a common template (and after training to align personal True North to replace position descriptions).
To equip	• All teams to take part in the Everyone Coaches workshop to equip them for performance conversations.
	• All managers and team leaders to be trained in three basic tools: (1) how to GET a Feedback Expectation, (2) replace position descriptions with a personal True North, (3) Speed Review.
To partner	• True North and GET Feedback Expectation to be confirmed for all staff.
	• Speed Review templates to be customised to suit business units.
	• Feedback circles and REAL conversations to be facilitated as the prescription takes effect.

'I totally agree', said Ralph. 'People can do really effective reviews on a blank sheet of paper, while others have the world's latest technology and can't make it work at all, so if *cure the review* gives people the confidence to invite and accept the truth, then this will be more than enough.'

you *can* handle the truth

Just before he was due to leave for the airport Ralph took Santa aside. 'I just wanted to thank you for having the courage to tell me the truth. It's not easy in my position to get anyone to level with me, but you did and you did so in a way that made things better.'

'Thank you', replied Santa.

'Now, I'm still a grumpy over-achieving businessman, so I'll be back in three months to see if you and Georgie can actually deliver on your promise.'

Santa smiled. There was a massive amount of work to do to get Santa Enterprises and Donut Delicacies on the right track, but he knew exactly what needed to be done.

He looked forward to seeing Ralph Hampton Jr in three months. There was nothing to fear now. He was ready to become the man who cured the performance review.

chapter 16

cured!

Four months after the momentous meeting in Lapland, the XFS executive team and two guests met in New York for the quarterly PDCA meeting.

A plate of donuts sat in the middle of the expansive table.

Occasionally someone muttered to the person next to them. Mostly it was silent and tense.

Santa looked longingly at the donuts, but the lemon detox diet had been great so he didn't want to go back to the old days of being overweight.

'Go on, just one, GM', prodded his cheeky companion. 'That won't do any damage.'

A door swung open and Ralph Hampton Jr emerged waving a large piece of paper. 'Look at this', he yelled. 'Unbelievable!'

People tried to see what was on the sheet, but Ralph was waving it wildly as he called out, 'Twenty-two per cent increase in productivity in three months. Cost savings greater than the past year put together. Staff turnover close to zero. Customer satisfaction through the roof!'

Santa smiled. 'Not too difficult when you get back to basics', he thought. 'Just do your job, support your team, serve your customer and be engaged.'

Brad and Phil couldn't have looked more relieved if they'd won the lottery, and Ralph just stood there still waving those all-important results with one hand and feeding himself a donut with the other. Ralph was in heaven.

lapland

In just three months *cure the review* had swept across the two companies and by the end of six months its effect was profound.

With help from Bec Arthur, facilitator of the Everyone Coaches program, the great man and Georgie made sure that all the templates, modules and tools were designed and rolled out to hit Santa Enterprises and Donut Delicacies in a way that minimised their downtime from work, but maximised the impact on business performance.

The first part of the process was True North, which took the complex XFS business plan and put it into a form that everyone could actually understand. Now even the ever-suffering IT department had alignment of priorities from the business units back into their teams, projects and development plans. Friction disappeared as people found a common language and direction, and realised what was expected of them.

Everyone Coaches was rolled out in the first four weeks, with accompanying business projects that immediately delivered performance improvements. Brad watched with excitement as coaching behaviours turned problems into opportunities, and managers into coaches. He could see the confidence growing as people wanted to help each other to improve instead of resenting others' suggestions and comments.

Simultaneously, the complexity of job descriptions fitting to goals, which fitted to KPIs, which fitted to development plans and so on became simply Align. The GET a Feedback Expectation workshop attended by all staff not only resulted in goals that were clear, but also in expectations that sounded like partnering instead of status wars, and in a new level of trust where people no longer feared the dreaded performance review being used as weapon.

Feedback Circles, made famous in Santa's mind by the Queen, were facilitated by Bec and her team for all management teams down to team leader level by the end of the first quarter. Ted remained in the business largely because Santa and Brad used the REAL Scripts to have the tough conversation that was long overdue.

Amazingly, as Ted's Sleigh Maintenance team learned to get past the fear of feedback, they were the ones who transformed him. He even apologised to Matt and they were last seen happily working together on a new propulsion system.

Speed Review was simply a sensation. From the first group that was coached in how to use the tool the managers and staff alike agreed that this simple process blew away countless problems.

Not all was easy or perfect. It took people a while to get used to the Feedback Circles and to inviting their staff and colleagues to give them feedback. But no-one was the same and neither was the business. By the end of six months the monthly speed review and the whole emphasis on inviting feedback had done exactly as Santa and Georgie had predicted. It made the old performance review obsolete because the feedback had already been given, the changes made and people had moved on.

Managers and staff actually enjoyed the six-monthly Performance and Development Plan discussion. Ralph was right. It had gone from review to preview. The old review was dead.

orlando, florida

Georgie and Santa sat with Phil in the staff canteen at Donut Delicacies.

'I got it all wrong', Georgie said, picking up and studying an orange donut. 'I was convinced that the answer to curing the review was to get people to focus on the donut, not the hole. That seemed so simple. But you've got to deal with the truth not just look at the sugar and sprinkles. There is a hole and without it you don't have a donut.'

'Yeah,' reflected Santa, 'the donut is a great way to remind you that the problem with the performance review wasn't really about the process, it was about performance conversations or lack of them. Half the people were just talking about the hole and being too negative, and the other half were just talking about the sugar and sprinkles. To cure the review you have to do both; you have to handle the truth.'

'Oh, well, enough about donuts and holes', said Georgie. 'I'm still waiting to find the right guy, and now that we've cured the review I can spend more time on that.

'So, what's next for you, GM?'

'Oh I've got plans to …'

Santa's phone started ringing, interrupting the conversation. 'It's for you, Georgie. A guy called Todd from England. Says he's calling to ask you out on a date.'

'Yoo hoo!' cried Georgie, dancing out of the canteen with Santa's phone to her ear.

'That's good luck, isn't it?' Phil said to Santa as they stood to leave.

'Perhaps', said Santa, smiling.

'What do you mean?', asked Phil, somewhat intrigued. 'You didn't call that guy and set that up did you?'

'Let's just say that it's amazing what can happen when you have a *real* conversation.'

epilogue

The story finished an hour out of Los Angeles and I hadn't slept a wink but that didn't matter.

'What do you do for a living?' the American asked. It was a question that I had ducked earlier to avoid upsetting his storytelling.

'I write business novels and design development programs', I replied with a wry smile.

'Really! In that case, would you be interested in writing the story of the man who cured the performance review?'

'Absolutely!'

'Great. Let me give you my card', he said, reaching for a folio.

'You're Brad Smyth, aren't you?', I ventured.

'What makes you think that?' he laughed.

'Well, for a start, we're not in business class, you sound like someone who believes in the things that he does and you know the story intimately.'

'Nice guess', he laughed, handing me a business card with a bright orange donut. I read the name. Ralph Hampton Jr.

'Why aren't you in first class?', I asked, gobsmacked to be sitting next to one of the richest men in the world and not exactly the hero of the story.

'When you get feedback from Santa Claus it kind of changes your life', he replied.

'Sure,' I laughed, 'but Santa Claus isn't real so where did the story come from?'

The speaker overhead crackled, 'Ladies and gentlemen, please fasten your seat belts ...'

The flight attendant hovered over me, 'Sir, you slept through breakfast so I hope you don't mind that we didn't wake you.'

I looked at the man next to me. It wasn't the American. He was wearing a neat pair of slacks, fashionable striped shirt and blue blazer, which made him look like any other middle-aged traveller of some wealth. His hair was white, and he had a ruddy complexion and engaging smile.

He smiled and handed me a card.

On it was an orange donut and the name Mr San Taclaus.

I looked at him. It couldn't be. I took a deep breath and asked the second most obvious question: 'Are you the man who cured the performance review?'

He just looked at me and laughed: 'Ho, ho, ho!'

the cure the review™ framework

The performance review must surely be one of the most sacrosanct of all business processes because it remains an unchanging feature of the majority of organisations despite its cost, limited value and almost universal ridicule.

Certainly the three basic aims of the review make sense:

- align individual behaviour with business direction
- provide feedback
- discuss and define career goals and development plans.

Unfortunately somewhere along the way people got the idea that this could all be accomplished in one meeting every six or twelve months, backed by a clever recording system and a raft of HR processes and guidelines. Not only is the performance review ineffective in achieving these aims, but it can be directly or indirectly responsible for damaging relationships, reducing openness, instilling mistrust and even increasing staff turnover while achieving little.

The time is right to find a better way. We need to replace the bureaucracy with a simpler process that aligns the business goals with the individuals who actually do the work and fosters a culture of performance conversations. To achieve this means reducing the fear of feedback and developing people with the skills to invite, accept and offer effective two-way feedback.

That 'better way' is described in narrative form as the prescription in the story of *The Man Who Cured the Performance Review* and through the cure the review™ framework on which the book is based.

Since creating the framework it has been inspiring to see organisations showing the courage to say 'Enough!' and replace the review (to the cheers of staff at all levels) with a real feedback process that is owned by the business instead of HR.

The following section describes the key elements of the cure the review™ 'prescription', answers some of the most frequently asked questions about the framework, and explains the services and resources that are available to help you to implement the cure. Further details are available at <www.curethereview.com>.

the prescription

The prescription addresses the three root causes of the failure of performance reviews to meet expectations — bureaucracy, ill-equipped people and fear of feedback. The details that follow outline the cure for each of the ills, as described in the story, and offer guidance in how to apply the three elements — align, equip and partner.

The prescription		
For bureaucracy: align	**For ill-equipped people: equip**	**For fear of feedback: partner**
True North	Invite Feedback	Feedback Expectation
PDCA Cycles	Receive-Reflect-Respond	Feedback Circles
Principles of Align	REAL and RITE scripts	Speed Review

the cure for bureaucracy — align

The word 'align' summarises perfectly how to tackle the bureaucracy that has overwhelmed the review. Align means creating a clear sense of purpose, making the system people-friendly, minimising detail and getting away from the 'tick and flick'.

Three elements are part of this—True North, PDCA and Principles of Align.

true north

Most companies have a strategic plan and/or business plan, but rarely does it mean much beyond the senior management ranks. Accordingly, this first part of the prescription is to create a simple yet effective frame on which people from every level—from whole-of-business to teams and individuals—can answer the four fundamental questions:

- Why are we here?
- What must we achieve?
- How will we achieve those things?
- What values and principles will guide us?

These frames can be facilitated for teams in half-day sessions and are a great way to build ownership. It is then an easy step to apply the same process for individuals and align through the team goals to the business goals.

PDCA

The simple Plan–Do–Check–Adapt cycle that is based on W Edwards Deming's original model describes the performance loop, which, ironically, is what is supposed to happen in the so-called performance management cycle. A key to the success of the 'cure' is to get in synch with the two PDCA cycles which are a natural feature of the performance planning process in any well-run business.

Cycle one is the short-term weekly, monthly and quarterly *review* of performance against the plan, while cycle two is six- to twelve-monthly and puts emphasis on *preview* by defining strategies, setting goals and determining the actions and accountabilities for the next period.

The cure the review™ framework aligns with these two PDCA cycles:

- *Cycle one.* This involves regular day-to-day feedback with the pivotal event being the one-on-one partnering review meeting between team leaders and their direct reports for twenty to thirty minutes every four to eight weeks using the Speed Review template. This ensures efficient and productive performance conversations that will add value to the business.

- *Cycle two.* The six- to twelve-month cycle, which tackles job and career development, is usually well-supported by the existing performance review forms and system; however, the True North and

Feedback Expectation tools simplify and maximise the value of this process.

principles of align

It is often best to avoid the words *performance review* and *performance management* because of their negative connotation and simply replace them with *align* because that is precisely what you want to achieve. The key Principles of Align are not an exhaustive or prescriptive list, because one of the aims of cure the review™ is to dovetail into the existing system and not force organisations to replace what they have already created or installed.

The key Principles of Align that should be considered are as follows:

- The purpose of Align is to optimise people performance and development.

- Align is built on two PDCA cycles — one- to two-monthly partnering review and six- to twelve-monthly preview.

- Begin with a feedback expectation between manager and staff as partners.

- Mandatory partnering reviews should be part of managers' KPIs.

- The success of Align depends on equipping people to have REAL conversations.

- Align is owned by the business units not HR.

- Align should operate on an administration platform that suits the culture.

- Invite feedback — make surveys, feedback loops and debriefing part of the day-to-day business.

the cure for ill-equipped people — equip

The concept of Everyone Coaches has been something of a revelation for many organisations and their teams. Not only does it give people the skills and confidence to have the feedback conversations, but it also equips them with life skills that are extremely valuable for parenting and in other interpersonal roles. The three core elements are Invite Feedback, Receive–Reflect–Respond, and REAL and RITE Scripts.

invite feedback

While researching performance reviews one of the real 'aha!' moments was when my team and I realised that the fundamental premise of giving feedback was wrong and that we needed to turn that on its head and put the focus on inviting feedback.

It is amazing to see how the fear of feedback subsides and the truth emerges as people get more skilled and comfortable in inviting feedback instead of having the pressure to push feedback on to others.

receive–reflect–respond

To become skilled and confident in inviting feedback requires the ability to accept the information in a way that encourages people to keep the feedback coming.

This takes time and practice because the natural tendency is to react instead of reflect. This is more about emotion than logic, but as people learn that feedback can be valid, fuzzy or invalid, and it is their choice how to respond, there are fewer emotional reactions and there is greater learning.

The use of coaching ploys such as the yoyos is an effective way to depersonalise feedback while people get through the early stages of learning how to receive it.

REAL and RITE Scripts

The simple REAL and RITE Scripts provide an easy tool to plan performance conversations and also to handle the spontaneous situations. Behind both tools is the key to all feedback: making it direct, specific and behaviour-changing or behaviour-reinforcing.

The formats for REAL and RITE are explained in the story, but the key points are:

- focus on specific behaviour (what really happened)
- describe the effect or impact
- explore if the person understands
- leave people looking forward after giving some' tough love'.

We have successfully coached hundreds of business leaders and team members in how to use the REAL Scripts to tackle those tough conversations that are a part of business and personal lives. More detail on this approach is available at <www.curethereview.com>.

partner

The fear of feedback is arguably the elephant in the room when it comes to the root causes of ineffective performance management systems. This underlying fear is one of the reasons the processes used by businesses have become more and more bureaucratic, as they seek to almost entrap managers and team leaders to give feedback. Unfortunately this has had the opposite effect and simply reinforced the 'dancer and dumper' behaviours described in the story.

The fundamental way to get past the fear of feedback is to do it early and do it often as part of a partnership. The three elements of building and sustaining that partnership are Feedback Expectation, Feedback Circles and Speed Review.

feedback expectation

The concept of feedback expectation seems so obvious to sportspeople and yet it is missing from most businesses.

Mr Peng summed-up this concept perfectly: 'If you want to cure this fear of feedback, then create a strong partnership between the manager and direct report, and between colleagues. That partnership is what you might call a "feedback relationship" because both partners want and expect feedback from each other.'

To create the feedback expectation use the GET tool (goals, expectations, trust) because this provides the essential clarity of expectations on which partnering is built. Our experience suggests that there is enormous value in coaching managers and team leaders to create a feedback expectation because without it there is no basis for a partnering relationship in which people openly speak the truth.

feedback circles

Of all the elements in the prescription, Feedback Circles is the one that we call 'advanced' because it is most effective (and lower risk) once people have become accustomed to working in an environment where feedback flows freely.

If you have read or implemented think one team™ you will be familiar with the concept of debriefing, which is a great way to get people to develop a high regard for regular, open feedback conversations. That sets the foundation for introducing Feedback Circles, which are team conversations in which people invite feedback from colleagues.

This is a powerful process because it actually does lead towards a team that has no fear of feedback, and that is an awesome thing to see!

speed review

The purpose of the Speed Review template is to provide a debriefing tool that guides the performance conversation. This is a fundamental part of the prescription because as people develop their templates and get used to using them, the openness of feedback between managers and direct reports can be genuinely inspiring.

The example in the story shows the basic four elements of the template for the direct report—do your job, serve your customer, support your team, be engaged—and the two elements for the manager—give direction and provide support.

There are many different and effective versions of these templates but they all focus on the six key elements, have minimal use of detailed rating or ranking systems, and foster an efficient and effective two-way conversation.

Having seen what an impact coaching people to use a Speed Review instead of the old performance review can have on a company it really makes you wonder why it has taken this long for such a system to be implemented.

frequently asked questions

The interest generated by cure the review™ has been quite amazing, and unsurprisingly people have lots of questions because we are tearing down a sacrosanct process that has remained almost unchanged for the past century.

Some of the most frequently asked questions are answered here. (Further information can be found at <www.curethereview.com>.)

Should the salary review remained linked to the performance review and preview cycles?

As disappointing as it may be for many people, the major variable that determines salary in most jobs is not performance but rather market demand. Accordingly, it makes sense to decouple the salary review from the performance review and preview processes. By all means retain a level of bonus that is aligned to performance, but to suggest that performance determines salary is simply not true in most cases.

Do we have to dump our existing performance management system to implement cure the review™?

No. Most businesses retain their 'architecture' but change the cycle times, the base templates and the behaviours. The key is to ensure that the people performance systems support the performance conversations.

How do position descriptions fit into the overall framework?

This is a great question because the 'PD' has become an administrative nightmare as jobs keep changing in nature. We have found it far more useful to replace the position description with a True North template that focuses on why the job exists, what needs to be achieved and how that will happen. It also stops the arguments about who is responsible for updating the PDs!

When are goals agreed on between team leaders and direct reports?

This should happen after the business planning process (in most cases annually) and we recommend using the GET templates as described in the story. Expectations between managers or team leaders and their direct reports should be two-way.

Should staff be trained in how to participate?

Yes. We usually introduce the 'cure' in teams so that people become accustomed to having performance conversations as a natural part of their workplace.

How do I handle difficult employee behaviour?

Unfortunately we can all expect to work with a few passive–aggressive, argumentative or overly nervous people. Three useful tactics in this situation are:

- using REAL Scripts because they help you to stay on track and not be distracted

- using the GET tool to pay particular attention to employee goals and expectations, which gives you a better chance of engaging with things that motivate them

- using HR specialists for advice on where to draw the line on acceptable and unacceptable behaviour (as defined by organisation values).

Is there a place for 360-degree feedback in the PDCA cycle?

Definitely. The more feedback loops you create the more people become comfortable and skilled in having open performance conversations.

How should development and career plans be addressed in the annual meeting?

Career development should be discussed in the context of the organisation's policies and current situation. Encourage employees to articulate clearly their aspirations and help them to consider how they might achieve those goals. This means using your questioning and listening skills to help them to define issues such as training needs, the match between their ideal roles and their aptitudes, abilities, interests, and the possible pathways that will develop their skills and knowledge. Avoid pouring cold water on their aspirations, but encourage realistic short- to medium-term planning.

Should we still use a rating system as part of the review–preview cycle?

The use of scales such as 'exceeded expectations' is useful, but absolute numbers, such as 3.5, suggest a level of objectivity that simply isn't possible. In some settings (with effective leadership) this can have value but more often the ratings lead to cynicism and disengagement.

What if managers or team leaders claim they are too busy to do the speed review?

Just about every good manager or team leader that we came across while developing cure the review™ already had regular one-on-ones. They found the time because it was a priority and it delivered value. Accordingly, make the one-on-one a KPI for all managers and team leaders because it is definitely a 'best practice' that delivers value.

resources and services

The cure the review™ framework is offered as a series of facilitated development modules and related development tools and support resources that can be accessed through Graham Winter Consulting, our network of accredited facilitators or through in-house customisation and certification. In addition, our team provides facilitation and coaching on issues that are important to creating and sustaining the benefits of a genuine feedback culture.

what are the core modules?

The key elements of the prescription are available in modularised workshop format, and can be customised to suit existing programs and systems. These include:

- Aligning to True North—how to align business plans with individual behaviours

- Everyone Coaches—how to invite, accept and offer feedback

- REAL Scripts—how to tackle the tough conversations

- Speed Review—the art of regular two-way performance conversations

- Partnering—how to create and sustain the feedback expectation

- Feedback Circles—facilitated performance conversations for teams.

More details are available at <www.curethereview.com>.

what resources support the program?

cure the review™ is backed by practical resources including this book, extensive resource guides, simple and effective surveys, and a range of templates and tools to make it easy to implement the framework:

- *The Man Who Cured the Performance Review.* This book is a quick, powerful and cost-effective way to introduce the cure the review™ framework and the concepts of performance conversations to every employee in your organisation.

- *cure the review™ resource guides.* During the workshops comprehensive resource guides are provided to every participant. These guides provide the tools and instruction that is needed to implement the framework.

- *cure the review™ surveys.* The base online survey titled Review the Review gives a snapshot of employees' views on the current performance review practices. This is an effective way to identify the ills and plan for the cure.

Other surveys and related tools are available online to support the implementation of cure the review™.

why cure the review™?

The performance review is one of great remaining sacred cows of the business world and it has spectacularly failed to deliver the essential feedback loop between business performance and individual performance.

At last there is an alternative! This book and the innovative and practical tools that are available in the cure the review™ framework provide managers, team leaders and staff with the concepts and tools they need to plan for and hold the essential performance conversations.

cure the review™ enhances productivity and staff engagement by aligning the business and its people, creating a feedback expectation and bringing people together to invite, accept and offer the truth.

Graham Winter and his team can be contacted for further details through <www.curethereview.com>.

curethereview™